# MODELS OF THEOLOGICAL REFLECTION

Raymond F. Collins

UNIVERSITY
PRESS OF
AMERICA

LANHAM • NEW YORK • LONDON

Copyright © 1984 by

University Press of America,™ Inc.

4720 Boston Way
Lanham, MD 20706

3 Henrietta Street
London WC2E 8LU England

All rights reserved
Printed in the United States of America

**Library of Congress Cataloging in Publication Data**

Collins, Raymond F., 1935–
   Models of theological reflection.

   Includes bibliographical references and index.
   1. Pastoral theology–Catholic Church. 2. Catholic
Church–Doctrines. 3. Theology–Methodology. I. Title.
BX1913.C614   1984   253'.01'8      83–21733
ISBN 0–8191–3661–1 (alk. paper)
ISBN 0–8191–3662–X (pbk. : alk. paper)

All University Press of America books are produced on acid-free
paper which exceeds the minimum standards set by the National
Historical Publications and Records Commission.

In grateful memory
of
Gus and John
who introduced me
to ministry
and
reflection thereon

*Nihil Obstat:*   Rev. Msgr. Arthur T. Geoghegan, S.T.D.
                 *Censor Deputatus*

*Imprimatur:*    +Most Rev. Louis E. Gelineau, D.D., J.C.L., S.T.L.
                 *Bishop of Providence*
                 *September 6, 1983*

   The Nihil Obstat and Imprimatur are official declarations
   that this material is free of doctrinal or moral error.
   They do not imply any endorsement of the opinions and
   statements contained in the work.

The author wishes to express his gratitude to the following for
permission to make use of excerpts taken from their works:

The Crossroad Publishing Company, for the use of *Theological
Investigations,* Volume 11: *Confrontations,* by Karl Rahner
(c, 1974, by Darton, Longman & Todd, Ltd.).

The diocese of Providence, for the use of *Parish Renewal: Models
for Sharing Christ's Mission in the Parish,* edited by John
Dreher (c, 1974).

Doubleday and Company, Inc., for the use of *Models of the Church:
A Critical Assessment of the Church in All Its Aspects,* (c, 1974)
by Avery Dulles, and *Models of Jesus* (c, 1981) by John F. O'Grady.

The Macmillan Publishing Co., Inc., for the use of *The Priest as
Manager,* (c, 1969) by Arthur X. Deegan.

*Theological Studies,* for the use of "Mission: The Symbol for
Understanding the Church Today," by Roger D. Haight (c, 1976).

The United States Catholic Conference, for the use of *The Program
of Priestly Formation* (3rd. ed., c, 1981).

Table of Contents

# Preface

The reflection which follows, as indeed all reflection, has its own history. Like much other reflection, it is a response to an experience which I have had. In the awareness that this experience is not solely my own, I share this reflection with those who care to read these pages.

In part the reflection was prompted by a request made of me by the Rev. Robert Beloin, then director of Louvain's American College Theological Institute (ACTI) in mid-winter of 1980. He asked that I conduct a week long session on the topic of theological reflection for priests who were about to come to Louvain to participate in a theological enrichment program. Fr. Beloin had no concrete suggestion as to the content of my presentation but had suggested the topic because he was well aware that "Theological Reflection" was being promoted as an important ministerial skill in the United States and elsewhere. Although the subject was topical and the practice of "theological reflection" had already been introduced into many seminary programs of pastoral formation, there seemed to be little consensus as to the precise nature and purpose of the skill. Moreover, literature on the subject, particularly in its more philosophical and theological dimensions, was almost non-existent. Since then this lack has been partially filled by the publication of an excellent work by James D. Whitehead and Evelyn Eaton Whitehead, *Method in Ministry: Theological Reflection and Christian Ministry*[1]. Nonetheless my approach to the topic remains distintively my own. To some extent it is complimentary to the work undertaken by the Whiteheads and their associates, and I would recommend that their volume be read alongside my own reflections.

More generally, my thoughts on theological reflection have been prompted by my own experience of the so-called ministerial crisis. On the one hand, and particularly in Roman Catholic circles, the crisis is experienced in a lack of vocations and the lack of "quality" vocations. On the other hand, the crisis affects those who are actively engaged in the ministry. In the sixties, it was fashionable to speak of the "identity crisis" which men in priesthood and men and women in religious life were experiencing. Talk about the minister's identity crisis passed with the passing of the sixties, but the crisis continues insofar as those who are engaged full-time — and, to some lesser extent, those who are engaged on a part-time basis—in the ministry ask about the meaning of the tasks in which they are spending their lives' energies. Sometimes queries as to meaning arise from the minister's own self-awareness, from his or her own quest for meaningful personal existence. Sometimes the questioning arises from a need to explain the ministry to those "outside".

This latter point of view was reflected in the title of a short article by H. Paul Satmire, "We Really Need to Know What Pastoral Counselling Is —Reflections for Colleagues in Other Disciplines".[2] It is my conviction that it is not only the specificity of pastoral counselling which needs to be expressed. Rather what needs to be understood and expressed is the nature of the ministry itself. It is unto this end that I have embarked on the following reflections.

It is, of course, evident that no man walks alone. It is certainly true that my first steps were not unattended. Moreover the path which has led to this book is not one which I have trod alone. I have been fortunate to have been involved in the pastoral ministry on more than one continent. I have been just as fortunate to have been engaged in theological reflection in the United States and Europe, and to have dialogued with not a few Christians from Africa, Asia, and the Pacific South West.

I am grateful to all those to whom I have been called to minister, and who have ministered to me even as I have ministered to them. I am likewise grateful to all those whose thought has enriched and furthered my own, not only those authors whose names are cited in the pages which follow, but also those priests who asked the provocative questions during the American College Theological Institute sessions in 1980 and 1981 and those students whose prodding urged me to verbalize my thoughts in as concise a fashion as possible. No less am I grateful to the friends who sustained me throughout the work, in particular to those friends whose own stories of faith are partially reflected in these pages. A special thanks, however, is owed to Bob Beloin who asked me to blaze a trail and to Mrs. Ruby Wong who was responsible for the charting of the path.

Raymond F Collins<br>
Easter, 1983

1. New York: Seabury, 1980.

2. *Pastoral Psychology* 29 (1981) 244-253.

# Part One

# The Nature and Purpose
# of
# Theological Reflection

Chapter One

Pastoral Theology and

Theological Reflection


Among the branches of theological science,
pastoral theology is a relatively new discipline.[1]
Indeed, Anton Graf (1811-1867), the Tübingen theologian,
was one of the few nineteenth century theologians to
develop systematically a notion of pastoral theology.[2]

Today there are still some who consider pastoral
theology to be merely the *practicum* which ought to
accompany the formal theological studies of those who
are preparing for the ordained ministry. As such,
pastoral theology consists principally in the
acquisition of certain skills deemed useful for the
ministry. The content of pastoral theology is then
seen as a matter of technique. At most pastoral
theology can be called an art; for it hardly deserves
the name of a science. To the extent that this
understanding represents the true appreciation of
pastoral theology, pastoral theology is best left in
those fora where skills are acquired; it does not
belong in the university nor does it deserve a place
alongside the traditional theological disciplines
(Scripture, systematic theology, Christian ethics,
Church history).

Thus, throughout the nineteenth century and
during most of the twentieth century, pastoral theology
was considered to be a how-to-do-it course for those
soon to be involved in the practice of pastoral
ministry. In this same era ministry was largely
regarded as the private preserve of those who were
ordained. The declarations of Pius X on the lay
apostolate[3] served to entrench this view of ministry.
Pius taught that the lay apostolate was "the
participation of the laity in the apostolate of the
Church's hierarchy." The lay apostolate was the
assistance which the laity gave to the hierarchy in
order to assist them in their ministry.

With ministry thus construed as a clerical preserve, it was a simple step for pastoral theology to focus upon the skills to be acquired by those who were to be engaged in the pastoral care of souls. In seminaries and similar houses of formation, pastoral theology was directed to those who were one day to be charged with the *cura pastoralis*.[4] Pastoral theology was for those called to be pastors. Since sermons were preached by priests, homiletics was seen to be a branch of pastoral theology. Since the Mass and the sacraments were celebrated by priests, pastoral theology included pastoral liturgics (but this course was oftentimes not much more than a course in how to follow the rubrics found in the approved liturgical texts). Practical instructions for catechetics and other ministerial activities were also summed up under the rubric "pastoral theology". At bottom, however, pastoral theology was a matter of practice, of guidelines, of instructions, and of rules to be put into practice.

This view of the task of pastoral theology was clearly reflected in the opening words of the sixth chapter of the Second Vatican Council's *Decree on Priestly Formation* (October 25, 1965): "That pastoral concern which should thoroughly penetrate the entire training of seminarians also requires that they be carefully instructed in these matters which have a special bearing on the sacred ministry, especially catechetics, preaching, liturgical worship, the conferral of the sacraments, works of charity, the duty of seeking out the straying sheep and unbelievers, and other pastoral obligations. Let them receive careful instruction in the art of guiding souls, so that they can lead all the sons of the Church, before everything else, to a Christian life which is fully conscious and apostolic, and to a fulfillment of the duties of their state. With equal thoroughness they should learn to assist men and women religious to persevere in the grace of their vocation and to make progress according to the spirit of their various communities."[5]

An earlier paragraph of the same decree seems to reflect a somewhat different view of pastoral theology: "... theology should be taught in such a way that students will accurately draw Catholic doctrine from divine revelation, understand that doctrine profoundly, nourish their spiritual lives with it, and be able to proclaim it, unfold it, and defend it in their priestly ministry. ... ... Students should learn how these mysteries [of salvation] are interconnected, and be

4

taught to recognize their presence and activity in liturgical actions and in the whole life of the Church. Let them learn to search for solutions to human problems with the light of revelation, to apply eternal truths to the changing conditions of human affairs, and to communicate such truths in a manner suitable to contemporary man."[6]

This second view of pastoral theology is one which calls for the theology which has been learned to be integrated into the personal life of the minister; it also calls for theology to be related to the ministry in which he or she will be engaged. This view of pastoral theology, which relates theology to the minister and theology to ministry, is sometimes expressed in a curriculum which treats the pastoral implications of doctrine and tradition as a corollary to or an excursus upon an academic presentation of theology. Sometimes, however, this vision of pastoral theology is expressed in an attempt to permeate the entire gamut of theology with a pastoral perspective. While the permeation approach is certainly preferable in theory, it all too easily results in the reduction of theology to catechetics and of exegesis to the development of homiletic themes for the preacher.


### A New View of "Pastoral Theology"

There is, however, yet a third way of understanding pastoral theology.[7] This approach gives pastoral theology a role alongside that of the classical theological disciplines— Scripture, dogma, moral, and history—and defines its purpose as the "scientific and theological research into the task laid upon the Church in the present of achieving her own nature as Church."[8] In the view of Karl Rahner, a characteristic feature of pastoral theology, thus conceived, is that: "... it is not confined exclusively to the work of the clergy (and especially the 'lower ranks' of them) or to the 'cure of souls' exercised by these in the narrower sense of the term. Rather it extends to everything which the *Church* as such has to do, beginning from the worldwide Church and extending right down to the local churches and the local communities of believers. Thus... among questions pertaining to a pastoral theology of this kind would be, e.g., a scientifically conducted investigation into the form which a Roman congregation should assume today, where as a matter of concrete practice a balance can be struck between centralization and decentralization in the Church of today, how large a diocese ought to be today without having regard to the particular circumstances in particular societies in which it exists in any given case, what ecclesiastical institutions ought to exist at the supra-parochial level apart from the curia attached to the bishop of a diocese, what the constitution of a national conference of bishops ought to be. Such questions as this and others almost beyond number belong... to a pastoral theology of this kind because today these questions can no longer be left solely to the prudent estimation of the higher authorities of the Church or to mere practical experience to decide."[9]

Rahner has pleaded that "an exact scientific investigation... be made into the concrete situation of the Church both interior and exterior, since in practice the achievement of her own fullness depends upon this."[10] Such an investigation should certainly include an analysis of the historical and cultural factors which have contributed to shaping the concrete situation of the church today. Elements drawn from the study of biblical, ecclesiastical, and secular history can clarify the situation of the church of our times. No less illuminating will be insights into the contemporary ecclesial situation derived from the behavioral sciences. Clarification should be sought from this source since the church is composed of real men and women, even if they are men and women of faith. Since these men and women exist in different cultural contexts, a certain amount of cultural analysis can contribute to the investigation of the concrete situation of the church today. In this respect, philosophical thought, political interpretations, and the various religious traditions will be found useful in shedding light on the cultural context in which the church of a given locale takes concrete form.[11] If pastoral theology is conceived in this fashion it may well be that pastoral theology should be considered as a branch of fundamental theology.

Pastoral theology is a systematic and scientific reflection upon the concrete situation of the church, that is on the church as it is emerging in the actual exercise of its ministry. As such, pastoral theology is concerned with the praxis of the church, that is, in the words of David Tracy, "the critical relationship between theory and practice whereby each is dialectically influenced and transformed by the other."[12] Praxis lies somewhere between doctrine and practice. It is the touchpoint between *theoria* and

6

*pragma.*

One can approach the praxis of the church deductively. In this case one would draw a practical plan of action (ministry) from the insights and conclusions of systematic theology. The actual implementation of that plan is the church's practice, but the elaboration of the plan itself belongs to the domain of praxis. A typical development of a plan for ministry would include not only its pragmatic dimensions but also its theoretical underpinnings. One can, on the other hand, approach praxis inductively. One can attempt to elucidate the church's praxis by means of a systematic and scientific reflection upon the actual conduct of ministry by the church itself. Such an approach would appear to be consistent with the notion of pastoral theology proposed by Rahner. This approach is the method followed in the quest for models for theological reflection presented in these pages. To speak of an inductive method is generally to speak reductively; the present work, however, intends to bring the church's theory and its practice into a mutual dialogue so that the one can clarify and more effectively interpret the other.

With this understanding of the nature and task of pastoral theology we can appreciate the fact that pastoral theology not only draws from the traditional theological disciplines, but that it also informs them, both in the sense of providing information for their benefit, and in the sense of infusing them with a definite spirit and orientation. In this manner the relationship between pastoral theology and systematic theology is similar to that between biblical exegesis (and biblical theology) and systematic theology. Biblical exegesis is a resource for systematic theology which ought to be permeated with the spirit of biblical theology. Similarly, the scientific and systematic investigation of the concrete situation of the church is a resource for systematic theology which ought to be permeated with the spirit of pastoral theology. Analogously, pastoral theology also exists in a dialogical relationship with moral theology and liturgics.

In his exposition of the claims which pastoral theology makes upon the theological endeavor, Karl Rahner has highlighted the need for all the theological disciplines to be given a pastoral orientation. As a first, and almost obvious, point he has underscored the notion that pastoral theology must "constitute an

important and significant branch of study among the
other branches which are included in the theological
formation of future priests."[13]

The pastoral theology needed by the future priest
can not, however, be reduced to mere pragmatics. In
Rahner's words, "... it would be regrettable if even in
the formation of priests of this kind pastoral theology
were, in practice, to be reduced from the outset to the
specific department of 'practical work... , and if the
future priest were not made familiar with the other
problems which belong to pastoral theology on a modern
and more comprehensive view of what this means.
Attempts are constantly being made to educate the
members of a society to a point where they can become
active supporters of the life of the society equipped
with a critical awareness of the problems involved, and
moreover, they must become this (with the due and
necessary reservations) by scientifically thinking out
the problems involved.  On this view, then, every priest
too ought to have the sort of formation which does not
merely equip him to fulfill the immediate pastoral task
to which he will be committed, but also, and more than
this, to take an active share in the responsibility of
the Church as a whole in the process of achieving the
fulness of her own nature.  He should have a social and
political awareness sharpened by scientific training
with regard to the life of the Church *as a whole*.  He
should be able to contribute actively in his own way to
the great decisions of the Church, etc.  Now the
necessary equipment to do this could be imparted to him
through pastoral theology, provided that the true nature
of this is understood and realized to the full, and
provided that pastoral theology is not reduced simply
to the level of mere useful ideas and relegated to those
sub-disciplines which alone, so it is alleged, are
interesting and important for the normal pastor."[14]


## An Epistemology

If this newer and more complete notion of pastoral
theology is such that it be incorporated into the
seminary curriculum in order that the future pastor take
an active share in the responsibility for the Church as
a whole, then it would appear that pastoral theology is
not simply investigative, rather it must move beyond
investigation to judgment, decision, and action.

Since the object of pastoral theology is the concrete situation of the church, of which the experience of the one who does pastoral theology is a personally significant part, some notions drawn from the cognitional theory of Bernard Lonergan might prove to be of use in the development of a viable pastoral theology.[15] Permeating Lonergan's work is an analysis of judging and deciding. He has commented that: "When one is reflecting, weighing the evidence, judging, one is experiencing one's own rationality. When one is inquiring, understanding, conceiving, thinking, one is experiencing one's own intelligence. When one is seeing or hearing, touching or tasting, one is experiencing one's own sensitivity."[16]

Since one experiences one's self differently as one is experiencing, understanding, judging, and deciding, Lonergan's theory of consciousness focuses upon a transcendental analysis of the concrete personal subject as experientially (empirically), creatively (intelligently), critically (rationally), and responsibly (morally) conscious and operating. That this analysis is integral to Lonergan's own understanding of fundamental theology is confirmed in one of the opening paragraphs of his *Method in Theology*. Lonergan has written that "... different levels of consciousness and intentionality have to be distinguished. In our dream states consciousness and intentionality commonly are fragmentary and incoherent. When we awake, they take on a different hue to expend on four successive, related, but qualitatively different levels. There is the *empirical level* on which we sense, perceive, imagine, feel, speak, move. There is an *intellectual level* on which we inquire, come to understand, express what we have understood, work out the presuppositions and implications of our expression. There is the *rational level* on which we reflect, marshal the evidence, pass judgment on the truth or falsity, certainty or probability, of a statement. There is the *responsible level* on which we are concerned with ourselves, our own operations, our goals, and so deliberate about possible courses of action, evaluate them, decide, and carry out our decisions."[17]

Such an epistemological approach suits those involved in pastoral theology, both as an academic discipline and as a tool for pastoral ministry, because they should begin, according to the understanding of pastoral theology that we have articulated here, with a real experience of the church, that is the church in its concrete situation. It is their own experience of

9

church which they are called upon to investigate in a scientific and systematic matter. Lonergan's cognitional theory suggests that understanding lies at a different level from (and, I would add, is often subsequent to) experience. Now what the investigation of the concrete situation of the church should lead to is an understanding of the Church in its actual existence. Only then is one able to make a judgment about it and proceed to take responsibility for it by means of a decision as to the action to be undertaken.

Experience is always of the given. The experience of the church, the primary object of pastoral theology, represents the primary consciousness level of the concrete pastoral theologian who deals with the object of his discipline. It may be useful to distinguish between the immediate experience of the church, mediated through sensory contact with those who are the church (the concrete personal experience of the pastoral theologian), and a mediate experience of the church, which comes to the pastoral theologian through the testimony of others (oral reports, newspapers, television, and so forth). For the purposes of the present exposition however, both the immediate and the mediate experience of the church can be allowed to characterize the pastoral theologians' first level consciousness of the church. Because of this first level of awareness, the theologian is able to add a second and third level to his consciousness of the church, that is, he or she is able to understand and judge it in its concrete manifestation. It is at this level that one can most appropriately speak of pastoral theology as praxis, the point where theory and practice come into contact, mutually permeating one another. On the basis of this understanding and judgment, one is enabled to take responsibility for the church in its becoming.

## The Official Teaching of the Church

These few reflections portray, in very broad strokes, the context within which one can speak of theological reflection. The nature of theological reflection has already been suggested by what has been written, but one can move beyond these generalities to a description of theological reflection found in some of the Church's official documents. Insofar as I have been able to determine, the language of "theological reflection" was first officially introduced into Roman

Catholic circles in 1971 when the *Program of Priestly Formation* was published by the United States' National Conference of Catholic Bishops. The first part of the document treated "Professional Formation for the Priesthood". Its first two chapters dealt with the objectives of the program and its academic component. "Pastoral Formation" was the topic of the third chapter, whose third article was entitled "Objectives of the Field Education Program". Within the context the document stated: "One of the principal goals of a Field Education Program is to teach the seminarian the habit of theological reflection about the priestly mission."[18]

This brief statement which identified theological reflection as a skill and habit to be acquired by the candidate for priesthood prior to ordination was greatly expanded in the second (1976) and third (1981) editions of the *Program of Priestly Formation*. After reiterating the 1971 statement, the 1981 text has stated:

"... In the context of field education, theological reflection refers to that process by which they attempt to perceive how theology and the tradition of the Church shed light on various pastoral situations they have experienced, how God's saving power and presence are operative in these experiences, and what this means for their own life in Christ. Theological reflection is then an attempt to identify God's saving power and presence in the events of the daily lives of all people, in order to understand more clearly the mystery of life and grace and the demands of God upon themselves and the Church. Moreover, as the seminarians engage in their active apostolate, they will be forced again and again to consider how their pastoral activity fulfills the mandate of Christ, how the various forms of the apostolate establish and build up the Church among men and women, how the needs of the People of God are being met by their service and witness. As they do this, under the direction of supervisors with pastoral experience and theological competence, this academic work and the apostolate will reinforce one another, and they will recognize the theological disciplines as relevant to their mission. Working side by side with priests and other ministers who show forth the spirit of Christ will not only inspire the seminarians, but will also capitalize on the process of learning by example and identification, an aspect of education that has been profitably used in medicine and other professions, but seldom in theological education. Thus

the field education program can be the best integrating
force in the total formation process, manifesting and
increasing the relevance of theology and linking more
closely the apostolic and spiritual aspects of the
students" lives."[19]

The *Program of Priestly Formation* returned to the
subject of theological reflection at a later moment
when it noted that "All these ecumenical endeavors will
be especially fruitful and spiritually beneficial when
supported by personal and shared theological
reflection."[20]  Taken together, these several texts
propose that theological reflection is a pastoral
skill,[21] one of the first to be acquired by the future
priest.  According to the first edition, theological
reflection is related to priestly maturity and one's
spiritual training, whereas the third edition looks to
theological reflection as an integrating force in the
total formational process.  As described in these texts,
theological reflection attempts (1) to discern God's
presence and action "in the events of daily life of all
peoples" and (2) to consider how one's pastoral activity
fulfills the mandate of Christ.  Pastoral reflection,
moreover, should result both from individual effort and
from mutual activity.

While describing theological reflection as a
pastoral skill, the third edition of the *Program of
Priestly Formation* has identified two foci for
theological reflection, one more general and more
theological, the other more specific and more
ministerial.  In a general fashion, theological
reflection should be concerned with identifying God's
saving power and presence in the events of life.  To
this extent, theological reflection is a matter of
discerning "the signs of the times".[22]  More
specifically, theological reflection is concerned with
ministry and the church.  It seeks to ascertain just
how well the individual minister fulfills his
ministerial mandate, how ministry builds up the church,
and how the needs of people are met by the church's
ministry, as exercised through her ministers.

1. See Karl Rahner, "The New Claims Which Pastoral Theology Makes upon Theology as a Whole," in *Theological Investigations*, 11: *Confrontations*, 1 (New York: Seabury, 1974) 115-136, p. 116.

2. Anton Graf, *Zur praktischen Theologie, 1: Kritische Darstellung des gegenwärtigen Zustandes der praktischen Theologie* (Tübingen, 1841).

3. See the encyclical letters *Il fermo proposito* (June 11, 1905) and *Pieni l'animo* (July 28, 1906) in *The Papal Encyclicals 1903-1939*, ed. by Claudia Carlen (Raleigh: McGrath Publishing Co., 1981), pp. 37-44, 57-61. See further Pius XI's first encyclical letter, *Ubi Arcano Dei Consilio* (December 23, 1922) in *The Papal Encyclicals 1903-1939*, pp. 225-239; his March, 1927 *Discourse to Italian Young Women*; and, his November 13, 1928 *Letter to Cardinal Bertram on the Origins of Catholic Action*.

4. See K. Rahner, *art. cit.*, pp. 116-117, 121-122.

5. *Optatam Totius*, par. 19. See *The Documents of Vatican II*, ed. by Walter M. Abbott, S.J. (New York: Association Press, 1967) p. 454.

6. *Optatam Totius*, par. 16, in *Documents*, 451-452.

7. This view has been developed in the *Handbuch der Pastoraltheologie: Praktische Theologie der Kirche in ihrer Gegenwart*, 4 vols, ed. by F. X. Arnold et al. (Freiburg: Herder, 1964, 1966, 1968, 1969). See also, K. Rahner, *art. cit.*; *Idem*, "Pastoral Theology," in *Sacramentum Mundi*, 4 (New York: Herder, 1969), pp. 365-368; Heinz Schuster, "The Nature and Function of Pastoral Theology," in *The Pastoral Mission of the Church. Concilium*, 3, ed. by Karl Rahner (Glen Rock: Paulist, 1965), pp. 4-14.

8. K. Rahner, "The New Claims," p. 118.

9. *Idem.*, pp. 118-119.

10. *Idem.*, p. 119.

11. See J. D. Whitehead-E. E. Whitehead, *op. cit.*, pp. 20-21.

12. David Tracy, *Blessed Rage for Order: The New Pluralism in Theology* (New York: Seabury, 1975) p. 243.

13. K. Rahner, "The New Claims," p. 121.

14. *Idem.*, p. 122.

15. See Bernard Lonergan, *Introducing the Thought of Bernard Lonergan: Three Papers from 'Collection' with an Introduction by Phillip McShane* (London: Darton, Longman and Todd, n.d.). Basic sources for Lonergan's thought on the topic include *Insight: A Study of Human Understanding* (New York: Philosophical Library, 1958); *The Subject* (Milwaukee: Marquette University Press, 1968); "Faith and Beliefs" (a paper presented at the Annual Meeting of the American Academy of Religion, 1969); and *Method in Theology* (New York: Herder and Herder, 1972).

16. B. Lonergan, *Introducing the Thought*, p. 19.

17. *Idem.*, *Method*, p. 9.

18. *Program of Priestly Formation* (Washington: National Conference of Catholic Bishops, 1971), par. 98.

19. *Program of Priestly Formation* (3rd ed.: Washington, National Conference of Catholic Bishops, 1981) par. 197, p. 55. The paragraph was taken over from the second (1976) edition, with some editorial modification.

20. *Program of Priestly Formation*, 3nd ed., par. 324, p. 85.

21. The document suggests that the field education program consists of three elements: "classroom work", "active pastoral involvement", and, "theological reflection."

22. See John XXIII, *Pacem in Terris, passim; Lumen Gentium*, par. 4, in *Documents*, 201.

Chapter Two


The Church and Theological Reflection


Some years ago the need for reflection on the
church was affirmed, in no uncertain terms, by the
Jesuit patrologist, Walter Burghardt, who wrote that a
"basic need... of the contemporary Church is reflection,
on herself, on her doctrine, on her mission."[1]
Burghardt's assessment of the needs of the church in the
mid-sixties strongly echoed the words of Pope Paul VI
who described what he called an "act of self-examination
on the part of the Church"[2] in his first encyclical
letter (August 6, 1964) in these terms:

"We believe that it is a duty of the Church at the
present time to strive toward a clearer and deeper
awareness of itself and its mission in the world, and of
the treasury of truth of which it is heir and custodian.
Thus before embarking on the study of any particular
problem and before considering what attitude to adopt
vis-a-vis the world, the Church must here and now
reflect on its own nature, the better to appreciate the
divine plan which it is the Church's task to implement.
By doing this it will find a more revealing light, new
energy and increased joy in the fulfillment of its own
mission, and discover better ways of augmenting the
effectiveness and fruitfulness of its contacts with the
world."[3]

The need for theological reflection has therefore
been voiced clearly by theologian and pontiff alike, yet
one must take care lest one think that theological
reflection is a passive condition, as if reflection was
simply a matter of mirroring the church. This is far
from being the case. Paul VI spoke of the discovery of
better ways of augmenting the effectiveness and fullness
of the church's contact with the world as a by-product
of its reflection. Perception psychologists suggest
that perception should lead to behavior and becoming.
Indeed Lonergan's cognitional theory prompts us to
consider that the fourth level of consciousness is one
in which the conscious subject participates responsibly.
It is a level of consciousness that focuses upon
decision and action. Theological reflection should
therefore be seen as an investigation of the experience
of the church which allows those who participate in the

15

process to take responsibility for the church.[4]
Theological reflection bears the power to change the
church.

If theological reflection is both necessary for
the church[5] and a means of changing the church, it
almost goes without saying that theological reflection
is a function of the Church. Theological reflection has
and is an ecclesial function. If so, one should ask who
within the church is to do theological reflection.
Since theological reflection enables one to take
responsibility for the church, it is clear that those
who have responsibility for the church must engage in
theological reflection. Certainly one should think of
the hierarchy as having a responsibility to be involved
in the process of theological reflection. The members
of the hierarchy hold positions of leadership within the
church. They have a primary responsibility for the
church in virtue of the office and mandate entrusted to
them. The view that it is the hierarchy which has
particular responsibility for the church undoubtedly
prompted Rahner's assertion that pastoral theology, in
the sense which has been proposed, should be a part of
the seminary curriculum, that is, it should be part of
the formation of those who will enter into the
hierarchical leadership of the church through
sacramental ordination. A similar point of view was
represented in the National Conference of Catholic
Bishops' *Program of Priestly Formation.*

Theological reflection ought, therefore, to be
construed not only as an ecclesial function but also as
a ministerial function. Its aim is to enable the church
to be ever more true to itself, to help the church
fulfill its ministry and its mission in a way which is
ever more adequate and more complete.[6] Since
theological reflection is an enabling function within
the church, theological reflection ought to be done by
those who have as their primary responsibility to help
the church fulfill its mission. Theological reflection
is an essential component of pastoral ministry in the
traditional sense, that is the ministry of bishops,
priests, and deacons called to minister within the church
in order that the church fulfil its mission as
authentically and as fully as possible.

This notion of theological reflection as a
ministerial function is consistent with the view of
ministry proposed by Henri Nouwen[7] more than a decade
ago. Having analyzed the generation in which we live as
the inward generation, the generation without fathers,
and the convulsive generation, Nouwen described what is
to be expected of one who aspires to be a Christian
leader. Corresponding to his three-fold description of
our times, Nouwen proposed three characteristics of the
contemporary leader of the church. The church leader
must be an articulator of inner events, a person of
compassion, and a contemplative critic. While we cannot
afford to denigrate the pastor's need for compassion, we
should recognize that the ability to articulate the
meaning of inner events and the ability to criticize in
a contemplative and constructive fashion correspond to
the levels of understanding and judging in our
cognitional theory. In short, theological reflection is
a pastoral or ministerial skill. Clearly, then,
theological reflection belongs to the domain of pastoral
theology.

John Shea[8] has identified three loci of
ministerial theology: helping abilities, change agent
abilities, and theological abilities. As he has
described each of these loci, the need for theological
reflection becomes increasingly apparent. In Shea's
view of helping abilities as the first locus of
ministerial theology, the minister should (1) help the
helpee explore his/her feelings (empathy); (2) help the
helpee put his/her feelings in a larger context (self-
disclosure, immediacy, confrontation); and, (3)
facilitate action (development of action programs,
support). As a helper the minister is expected to
reflect on a given pastoral experience — in the typical
case, a given personal situation — in order to clarify
its meaning and thus enable the one involved, and
occasionally the minister as well, to react decisively
and responsibly.

Shea distinguished four stages in the minister's
change-agent abilities: diagnosis, goal-setting,
program-development, and implementation. In the
diagnostic stage, the minister analyzes the situation
and brings needs to the surface. In the goal-setting
stage, the minister formulates concrete, behaviorally
oriented goals. In the program-developmental stage, the
minister designs programs that will effectively achieve
these goals. Finally, in the implementation stage, the

minister carries these programs out and evaluates their effectiveness.

The scheme of cognitional theory which we have borrowed from Bernard Lonergan can help to clarify both the helping and the change-agent abilities of the minister. The skills required of the minister insofar as he or she needs helping abilities are in fact no different from those required by a counsellor in any of the "secular" fields of counselling, guidance counsellors, marriage counsellors, and psychological counsellors, for example. The change-agent abilities of the minister are similar to those of all community organizers. They can be found in politicians and business executives as well as in ministers and church leaders. In a word, helping abilities and change-agent abilities can be applied to quite a variety of contexts. They become components of a ministerial skill only when they are joined with a theological ability and exercised in relationship to an agenda which the theological ability of the minister carries. It is the theological ability of the minister which allow his/her counselling to be termed pastoral counselling. Similarly it is the theological ability of the minister which allow his organizational efforts to be considered as ecclesiastical organization. The perception of the function and its statement of purpose make the difference.

In Shea's analysis of the theological abilities of the minister, four activities are highlighted: (1) hearing the religious dimension of what is articulated in secular language and responding with Christian perception; (2) hearing the explicitly theological questions and responding to them with accurate theology; (3) hearing the assumptive world and responding by bringing this assumptive world to the surface; and, (4) hearing the relationship between the Christian story and responding to it in the formulation of programs. Thus the theological abilities required of the minister basically belong to the category of listening and response.

To what must the minister listen? Shea has suggested that the first sounds to which the minister must listen are sounds articulated in the secular language of our everyday experience. Immediately one can cite the pastoral situation in which a pastor must listen to those who are speaking about their loneliness or their disaffiliation. At bottom this language speaks of a poor self-image, of little self-worth. The traditional theological categories appropriate to the experience are, among others, those of sin. To this the pastor can speak from the Christian religious tradition in terms of forgiveness and election, of love and community. To some extent this first theological task of the minister echoes Paul Tillich's method of correlation in the doing of theology.[9] Tillich held that theology is best done by bringing together the questions which arise in contemporary experience with responses which arise from the Christian tradition.

Yet there is more to the theological skill of the minister than merely explicating in Christian language ("understanding") the cries and questions of those who speak only the language of the world. The minister is also one who hears the explicitly phrased theological questions and appropriately responds to them. In the experience of the typical pastor of our times, the explicit theological questions which are raised often bear upon the significance of the traditional symbols of faith. "What is the meaning of the Resurrection?" "Was Jesus truly born in Bethlehem?"

Once this type of question has been responded to, the minister is called upon to listen to the assumptive world and to respond to it. Western society in the years following upon the Second World War dreamed that it was entering upon an irenic and utopic era. It was thought that once a few technical problems had been solved, the great society would be realized. Simultaneously a focus on the theology of hope emerged in the writings of academic theologians. In the study of Christian ethics and moral theology, agapé became the center of interest and the reality of sin all but passed from the formal agenda. Almost as a response there developed an obsession with the occult within secular society. Such novels and movies appeared as *The Exorcist* and *The Omen*. Was not this an indication that society had lost an ability to speak of the reality of evil? Might not the theological skills of ministers have led them to speak of the reality of sin in our midst in a more appropriate fashion?

Shea has also spoken of the minister's ability to hear the relationship between the Christian story and the world and to respond to it by developing programs. Once again the minister finds himself or herself engaged in the task of correlation. As the Christian narrator tells the story of Jesus who cured the sick and narrates the tale of the disciples who were engaged in a healing ministry and as that same minister observes a world in

19

which vast numbers are without adequate medical treatment, the narrator-become-minister might devise a program to bring both medication and medical care to those who are most in need of it.

## Ministry and Sacrament

An almost endless list of examples can be cited which would underscore the fact that theological reflection is a necessary pastoral skill. It is one of the primary aptitudes to be developed by those who aspire to positions of leadership within the church. Since theological reflection is designed to enable the church to "achieve the fulness of her own nature", theological reflection is necessarily a ministerial task.

It is difficult to adequately summarize a theology of ministry within a few words. Indeed one of the questions raised by students of sacramental theology within the Roman Catholic tradition concerns the specificity of the sacrament of orders. In my view, orders is a sacrament — distinct from the other six sacraments — insofar as it is the sacrament of ministry. Traditionally sacrament has been viewed as an efficient sign. The ordained minister, episcopal, presbyteral, or diaconal, is one who functions within the church as a sign that the church is ministerial. His role is to symbolize the ministerial nature of the Church itself. Yet the ordained minister is more than merely symbol. Through him is effected that which he symbolizes. Although there are several different ways in which one can evaluate the efficacy of ordained ministry, one of them surely bears upon the relationship between the ministry of the ordained ministry and the common ministry of the faithful. In this perspective, the specificity of the ordained ministry lies in the task of the minister of facilitating, coordinating, and catalysing the ministry of the ecclesial communion.

The notion that the ordained ministry, specifically that of priesthood, is ordered towards facilitating the ministry of other Christians has appeared in a number of recent church documents. For example, a study commissioned by the National Conference of Catholic Bishops in the United States speaks of the presbyter as a "director of ministries". The document states that "The priest — and on a broader scale the bishop — discovers that he has become the 'director of

20

ministries', a true spiritual leader of active
Christians rather than the only person in the parish or
the given apostolate to manifest spiritual initiative."[10]
In a similar vein the Canterbury statement of 1973
stated that "it is the role of the minister to
co-ordinate the activities of the Church's fellowship
and to promote what is necessary and useful for the
Church's life and mission."[11]  More recently Pope John
Paul II wrote that the ministerial priesthood "serves to
make the faithful aware of their common priesthood and
to activate it."[12]

The ordained minister has an enabling function
vis-a-vis the Church.  His ministry enables the church
to be a ministerial church.  In this way, as both sign
and means, the ordained ministry is a sacrament of the
Church.  Since, on the one hand, the function of the
minister is to be a facilitator of ministry, and thus
enable the ministerial church to become a ministerial
church, and since, on the other hand, theological
reflection, of its very nature, serves an enabling
function, it would appear that theological reflection
is an integral part of the pastoral or ministerial task.
In classical theological terms one could say that
theological reflection *convenit ministerio sacerdotali*.
Only by doing theological reflection can the pastor
truly serve the church in a responsible manner.


### The Responsibility of All the Baptized

While it is necessary to affirm that theological
reflection is an integral part of the ministerial task
which belongs to the ordained minister in virtue of his
ordination and calling, one must ask whether
theological reflection should be considered the proper
reserve of the pastor.  While the pastor might be called
to minister on a full-time basis, and while he has
received the sacrament of orders, is it not true that
baptism is the fundamental sacrament of ministry?
Are not all the baptized truly ministers of the Church?
Is not their ministerial function expressed liturgically
in the various roles which are assigned to the baptized
when the Christian community gathers together in
assembly for the Eucharistic liturgy?

It is my conviction that Baptism is *the* sacrament
of ministry within the church.[13]  All Christians are
deputed to serve by virtue of their baptismal
committment.  Accordingly, all baptized Christians

21

should engage in the task of theological reflection.
For the baptized, theological reflection is neither a
luxury nor an optional activity.  Theological reflection
is necessary for all the baptized since all the baptized
are called to participate in the life of the church in a
responsible fashion.  Because theological reflection has
responsibility for the church as its goal, all
Christians must participate in the process of
theological reflection.  Not to do so is sinful.
Although harsh, the statement can be made without
further qualification.  Irresponsible conduct is evil.
According to Aquinas' understanding of the natural law,
the fundament of moral reflection, the *bonum morale*
(moral good) was that which was according to reason and
therefore to be done, whereas the *malum morale* (moral
evil) was contrary to reason, and therefore to be
shunned.  Evil is a moral or ethical category; the
corresponding theological category is sin.

It goes without saying, of course, that many
baptized Christians actually engage in theological
reflection without calling their activity theological
reflection.  That this is so is no more surprising than
is the realization that there are many individuals who
think and judge, thereby taking responsibility for their
actions, without having formally studied either
epistemology or ethics.  In fact many baptized
Christians really do theological reflection without
using this technical terminology, indeed without being
able to systematically reflect upon and theologically
articulate what they are doing.  Such Christians would
certainly include those vast numbers of the faithful who
have to formulate priorities as to their own involvement
in the church and its activities.  They weigh their own
faith committment, their several obligations, and their
talents, and they try to reach a responsible decision as
to how best they might participate in the ministry of
the church.  Were their experience to be examined in
systematic and scientific fashion, one would have to say
that they were indeed involved in the process of
theological reflection.

When the baptized faithful begin to participate in
the ministerial task of theological reflection, they
often find that they are on a collision course with
those who are set over them as their pastors.
Frequently the expected collision is caused by the fact
that the pastor himself is not sufficiently involved in
the process of theological formation, if, indeed, he is
involved in it at all.  Nevertheless, despite the
possibility of confrontation between pastor and

faithful, it is necessary that the laity, as well as ordained ministers — in our times, especially the educated laity whose faith commitment should include the committment of their intellects to the Lord — participate in the process of theological reflection. When both clergy and laity are so involved, the total process will be both more complete and more effective. Indeed, the *Program of Priestly Formation* suggests that the process of theological reflection be both personal and mutual.[14] If theological reflection is "shared" effort, a joint endeavor by clergy and laity is certainly to be encouraged. In the past, "theology" was the profession of experts, but now theology must be done "after work hours" and in community. By mutual reflection greater light will be shed on the ministry of the church.

It is not pragmatic interests alone which dictate mutual reflection as the normative mode of theological reflection. The very nature of the sacrament of baptism points to the suitability (perhaps even the necessity) of joint theological reflection. For the laity to participate in theological reflection is a way for them to participate meaningfully in the life and ministry of the church. For the faithful, theological reflection is simply a matter of taking one's baptism seriously — and that all baptized Christians ought to do! On the other hand, when pastors and clergy do not appreciate the theological reflection of the faithful they are, in effect, demeaning the baptismal responsibility of the baptized. The clergy hardly have a monopoly on the Holy Spirit;[15] neither do they have a monopoly on theological insight. With Paul, each baptized Christian can say, "I think that I have the Spirit of God."[16]

The realization that theological responsibility is the common responsibility of all baptized Christians, albeit a particular responsibility of those called to specific leadership positions within the church, calls for some further precision of the notions which have been advanced so far. First of all, if the ordained minister is called to do theological reflection in view of his responsibility for the church, and if his ministerial function should enable the church to be ministerial, then one of the specific tasks of the ordained minister in the church is to facilitate the theological reflection of those members of the church who seek to make sense of their Christian lives. The ordained minister must not only do theological reflection; he is also called to be a facilitator of theological reflection.

A second corollary of the idea that theological reflection is the joint responsibility of leadership and membership within the church is that much of the terminology which has hitherto graced works in pastoral theology, and which the reader will find sprinkled throughout these pages as well, stands in need of some refinement. Rather than use the language of "pastoral theology", we should employ the terminology of "ministerial theology". "Pastoral theology" implies that this branch of the theological endeavor is limited to those who are engaged in the "pastoral care of souls". However all Christians have some responsibility for the church. The branch of the theological task to which the rubric "ministerial theology" appropriately applies is sometimes called "applied theology" or "practical theology". However, these terms do not convey the connotations of ecclesial mission and personal responsibility which are associated with the idea of "ministerial theology". Thus, we should consider theological reflection as an essential element of ministerial theology, a task to which each member of the church ought to be committed.

## Elements of Ecclesiology

Since ministry is a function of the church, it is obvious that a ministerial theology relates to the church. How one views ministerial theology depends on one's vision of the church (one's ecclesiology). How one does ministry depends on the type of church that one wants to construct. Thus one must affirm without any hesitation that ministerial theology is an ecclesial function. Indeed if ministerial theology is done at all, it is done in view of the church. One participates in the task of theological reflection in order that the church be faithful to itself, that it achieve the fullness of its own nature. The fidelity and growth of the church are the ultimate purpose of theological reflection. In sum, theological reflection is to be done in order that the church be and become church.

This brief statement of the purpose of theological reflection could not be made if one did not hold that ultimately theological reflection is a function of the church itself. There is an operative ecclesiology which permeates and inspires one's theological reflection. Some elements of the operative vision of the church which have shaped the notion of theological reflection suggested thus far are implicit in the first two

chapters of the present work.  It might be useful to
bring some of these elements to the fore and to identify
as the chief characteristics of our working
understanding, our "hypothesis", of the church the
following: (1) the church is the people of God,
(2) called unto mission, (3) in a dynamic fashion
(4) with a ministry which is largely exercised through
symbolic activity.  This is hardly an adequate
description, let alone an adequate definition of the
church, but it may suffice as an elementary statement of
an understanding of the church which the reader may
assume to permeate these pages.

First of all, The Church is the people of God.[17]
The operative theology of the present approach to
theological reflection is one which highlights a
populist ecclesiology.  This populist vision of the
church is one which is not only congenial to the
personalist philosophies and the democratic social
theories of our times, it is also deeply rooted in the
Christian biblical tradition and was recently reiterated
by the Magisterium of the church in a most solemn
fashion: "He planned to assemble in the holy Church all
those who would believe in Christ."[18]  A populist vision
of the church is one which uses the biblical images of
the People of God and the Body of Christ as the primary
analogues in ecclesiological reflection.  Such a vision
was confirmed by the Second Vatican Council[19] which
issued the *Dogmatic Constitution on the Church* on
November 21, 1964.  After an initial chapter on the
"Mystery of the Church", the *Dogmatic Constitution*
expatiated at length on the image of the church as the
People of God.[20]

A populist vision of the church is one which does
not denigrate the importance of the hierarchical nature
of the church.  Indeed a hierarchy is necessary for good
order and leadership within the church.  Nonetheless, a
populist vision of the church is one which underscores
the dignity of the individual believer in the corporate
body of the church and emphasizes the significance of
the activity of each believer within the life of the
church.  Accordingly a populist vision of the church is
one which highlights the importance of baptism[21] as the
rite of initiation into the church, as the fundamentum
of one's Christian dignity, and the source of one's
calling to the Christian life.  It is because of one's
baptism that one participates in the Eucharist, the sign
and symbol of the communion of the Church.

Secondly, the Church is called unto mission. This appreciation of the church also arises from a consideration of the Scriptures as well as from the study of official documents. The Gospel of Matthew is generally, and correctly, considered the most Church-sensitive of the four canonical Gospels. The first Gospel concludes in a dramatic scene,[22] when the disciples are sent forth into mission by the Risen Lord. That the church is essentially in the condition of mission was stressed by Vatican Council II's *Decree on the Church's Missionary Activity*.[23] The Gospel of Matthew and *Ad Gentes* express, as it were, a first moment and a last moment in the church's self-consciousness as a body of believers in mission, but this understanding permeates the church's entire history, and has given rise to a variety of "missionary" endeavors throughout the church's history. The significance of a missionary vision of the church has been noted by Roger Haight who has written that "one does not have to look hard to find a scriptural and traditional symbol responding to the question of the dynamic and functional relation of the Church to the World. The symbol is 'mission'. Mission theology is the one locus in ecclesiology that answers directly the function question of the church in the wider world context."[24]

Thirdly, to speak of mission is to suggest a notion of the church as a dynamic reality.[25] The church's being is in its becoming. The church is open to the power of the future. The church is sign, herald, and locus of the Kingdom[26] of God which, almost paradoxically, is but is not yet. To reflect thus on the nature of the Church as a dynamic reality is to suggest that the Church is an eschatological reality. Further reflection on this notion is best left to the ecclesiologists who have the ability and the forum to treat this characteristic of the church in an adequate manner. For the present purposes, it can simply be stated that the church is always in process. It is always in process because it is being brought ever into existence[27] through the power of the Spirit of God which is the power of God's future, the eschatological reality par excellence.

To reflect on the nature of the church as a dynamic reality simply in these traditional theological categories, with especial reference to the eschatological nature of the church is, however, hardly to do justice to the nature of the church itself. One can speak of the church as a theandric (divine-human)

26

reality. Accordingly one must pay attention not only to the divine power which calls the church into being and communicates its life and energy to the church; one must also be attentive to the human dimensions of the church. When one does so, one sees the dynamic nature of the church in yet another perspective. One could begin with the fact that the church exists in history. It is now, it always has been, and it will always be an historical reality. It is caught up in history. As history unfolds, so the church unfolds as part of history. This must need be since the church is alive, with a life which is both human and divine. As Newman said, "to live is to change and to be perfect is to have changed often."[28]

One might also consider the church as a human reality insofar as it exists only as a body of believers, as a group of men and women who interact with one another and with their culture(s). The membership of the church is comprised of human beings who must take hold of their own futures and shape them in responsible fashion. That "Grace builds on nature" (*gratia supponit naturam*) is an old theological adage. It reflects more than a modicum of truth. In regard to our present considerations, the truth of the adage signifies that the future of the church as a grace-filled reality is built upon the responsible decision of those who belong to the church and take responsibility for its future configuration.

To be sure, not all decisions taken by the membership (and/or leadership) of the church are fully responsible decisions. One who takes the church seriously must accept the fact of the sinfulness of the church. Luther spoke of the "church which is always to be reformed" (*ecclesia semper reformanda*). Because of the sin which adheres to its existence in the concrete circumstances of time and place, the church must always be reformed. It is called to be ever more faithful to the Gospel of Jesus Christ. Accordingly it is a church which is called to be a church ever caught up in the dynamic of a more complete faith response.

A fourth characteristic of the church which is the infrastructure of the present quest for a model for theological reflection is that a significant part of the church's ministry and activity is symbolic. That the making of symbols is, to a large extent, what the church's activity is ultimately all about is seen most clearly in the fact that to this day a large number of people believe that the principal activity of the church

is the celebration of the Eucharist. They see in the
celebration of the sacraments at least the paradigm, and
sometimes the very essence, of ministry. Indeed, one
might suggest that some of the movement within the
church on behalf of the ordination of women owes to a
sacramental view of the church, that is the notion that
ministry is validated and best expressed through the
celebration of liturgy and sacrament.

A comprehensive understanding of the nature of
ministry within the church does not limit even the
ministry of the ordained to their sacramental and
liturgical functions. Nonetheless there is another, and
more radical sense, in which one should approach the
symbolic nature of the church and its activity. In the
opening paragraph of the *Dogmatic Constitution on the
Church*, the Fathers of the Second Vatican Council
described the church as "a kind of sacrament or sign of
intimate union with God, and of the unity of all
mankind."[29] The language reflects the analysis of the
church by such leading theologians as Karl Rahner[30] and
Edward Schillebeeckx[31] who refer to the Church as a
fundamental sacrament. As Christ is the sacrament of
the encounter with God, the Church is the sacrament of
Christ. From a slightly different vantage point, and
reflecting the view of ecclesial sacramentality to which
the texts of Vatican II give witness, Richard McBrien
refers to the Church as the sign of the Kingdom of
God.[32] A view of the radical sacramentality of the
church was reflected in the programmatic encyclical
letter of Pope John-Paul II, *Redemptor Hominis.* In this
first encyclical the pontiff re-echoed the council and
repeatedly referred to the church as sacrament.[33]

Indeed the church is a sign or sacrament. It is a
sign of Jesus the Christ, it is a sign of the intimate
union with God and the unity of all humankind, it is a
sign of the reign of God. In short, the church is a
symbol, and its activities are to a large extent
symbolic activities. One can expand upon this notion by
saying that the activity of the church corresponds to
its nature. By nature the church is a sign; accordingly
its activity belongs to the order of sign. In its
activity the church manifests what it is. By what it
does the church symbolizes something of what it is.
Nonetheless by means of the very activity in which it
symbolizes what it is, the church is involved in the
process of becoming that which it is. The church's
self-expression is the means by which it becomes what it
ought to be.

One might draw an analogy between the church as the living Body of Christ and the human person. The human person is manifest to itself and to others in bodily form. Through its body it acts and interacts. The actions of a person correspond to personal existence, thereby manifesting what it means to exist in this world as a human person. For example, one eats because one is a corporeal existent. One talks because one is a social being. The activities of eating and speaking respectively manifest corporeality and sociality as aspects of personal existence in the world. However, these same activities are also the means by which personal existence grows and changes. One's physical makeup, one's size and shape, is modified by one's diet. One grows in one's social relationships and develops as a person by means of dialogue. Analogously the activities of the church are a sign of what it is and the means by which it grows and is transformed.

It is true that the church's sacramental activity, that is, the celebration of the seven sacraments, is one of the most characteristic, if not to say essential, activities in which it is engaged. According to classic Western theology, the celebration of the sacraments is activity in the mode of a sign. Yet even apart from the celebration of the seven traditional sacraments, most of the church's activity — integral to its well-being (its *bene esse*) if not absolutely necessary for its existence (its *esse*), and certainly characteristic of the church's present manner of being in the world — remains symbolic. In our time a most significant example of the church's symbolic activity has been the visits of Pope John Paul II to Mexico, Poland, Constantinople, Ireland, the United States, the Philippines, Japan, France, Great Britain and Argentina, Brazil and Central America. These visits are a symbolic expression of the universal pastorate of the Pontiff. On a much smaller scale the visit of a priest or Eucharistic minister to the sick is also a symbol of the church. Examples could be multipled at length; and each example would confirm the notion that the church's mission and growth is largely a matter of symbolic activity.

If the operative notion of church of which theological reflection is a function is that of a dynamic mission-oriented and symbol-making body of believers, then theological reflection can be legitimately brought to bear upon any reality which can be accurately described as ecclesial. When one thinks of church activity, one must think not only of the celebration of the sacrament within the Roman Catholic

Church, but of all activity which is constitutive of and
expressive of the church.  Thus "church" as used in
these pages can be applied indiscriminately to any body
of believers recognized as "church", the universal
Church, the Roman Catholic Church, the Anglican
Communion of churches, the local church (the diocese),
the parish, the domestic church (the Christian family),
and so forth.  All of these are so many expressions of
"church"; they are signs and symbols of that somewhat
abstract reality to which all too many theologians and
faithful refer under the rubric of "the church".  It is
the purpose of theological reflection to enable these
various expressions of church to become more fully
church by means of a systematic investigation of the
activities in which these "churches" express their
existence as churches.

1. Walter J. Burghardt, "Patristic Theology in an Ecumenical Age" (*The Eleventh Bellarmine Lecture,* October 19, 1966), *Theology Digest* 14 (1966) 271-283, p. 272.

2. Paul VI, *Ecclesiam Suam,* par. 19, in *The Papal Encyclicals 1958-1981,* 136-160, p. 138.

3. *Ecclesiam Suam,* par. 18, *Ibid.*

4. See K. Rahner, "The New Claims," p. 122.

5. See H. Schuster, "The Nature and Function of Pastoral Theology," p. 11.

6. *Idem.,* p. 7.

7. Henri J. M. Nouwen, "Christian Leadership of Tommorow," *Louvain Studies* 3 (1970-1971) 175-188.

8. See John J. Shea, "Doing Ministerial Theology: A Skills Approach," in *Towards Vatican III,* ed. by David Tracy (New York: Concilium, 1978) 188-195.

9. See Paul Tillich, *Systematic Theology,* 1 (Chicago: University of Chicago Press, 1951), pp. 3-68.

10. *Spiritual Renewal of the American Priesthood* ed. by Ernest E. Larkin and Gerald T. Brocolo (Washington: USCC, 1973), p. 16.

11. *Ministry and Ordination. A Statement on the Doctrine of Ministry Agreed by the Anglican-Roman Catholic International Commission. Canterbury 1973,* par. 7 in *Modern Ecumenical Documents on the Ministry* (London: SPCK, 1975), p. 32. See also par. 13, p. 35.

12. John Paul II, *Letter to All the Priests of the Church on the Occasion of Holy Thursday 1979,* 4 (Boston: Daughters of St. Paul, 1979), p. 15.

13. Commenting *Lumen Gentium,* pars. 10-13, Avery Dulles has written that "Art. 10-13 form a unit in which the Church is considered as reflecting in itself the triple office of Christ as priest, prophet, and king. This the Church does by its threefold function of worship (ministry), witness, and communal life. The present paragraph (*Lumen Gentium* 10) deals particularly with the priestly office.

The common priesthood of all the baptized provides the basis for, and requires for its completion, the ministerial priesthood of the ordained clergy." *Documents*, p. 27, n. 30.

Piet Fransen has written of "the apostolic mission common to all the members of the Church." See P. Fransen, "Orders and Ordination," in *Sacramentum Mundi. An Encyclopedia of Theology*, 4 (New York: Herder & Herder, 1969), 305-327. As a liturgical witness to this understanding of the function of the baptized, the first Eucharistic Prayer may be cited: "Father, we celebrate the memory of Christ, your Son. We, your people and your ministers... " See also *Les Sacrements d'Initiation et les ministères sacrés. Colloque de Tübingen organizé par l'Académie internationale des sciences religieuses* (Paris: Fayard, 1974), esp. pp. 201-202; Edmund Schlink, *The Doctrine of Baptism* (St. Louis: Concordia, 1972), esp. pp. 77-80.

14. The document speaks of "personal and shared theological reflection." See *Program of Priestly Formation*, 3rd ed., par. 324, p. 85.

15. "No one in the Church has a monopoly of the Spirit, who is given to each Christian according to his charge, his function and his personal vocation," writes Piet Fransen in "Orders and Ordination," p. 321.

16. 1 Cor 7:40.

17. See Avery Dulles, "The Church as Mystical Communion," Chapter Three of *Models of the Church. A Critical Assessment of the Church in all its Aspects* (New York: Macmillan, 1974), 43-57.

18. *Lumen Gentium*, par. 2, in *Documents*, p. 15.

19. Richard P. McBrien offers a summary overview of Vatican II ecclesiology in *Catholicism*, 2 (Minneapolis: Oak Grove, 1980), pp. 683-686.

20. Pars. 9-17, in *Documents*, pp. 24-37.

21. "Baptism is the beginning of everything, the source of all our obligations," writes Burkhard Neunheuser in "Baptism," *Sacramentum Mundi*, 1 (New York: Herder & Herder, 1968), 136-144, p. 139.

22. The Great Commission (Matt 28:16-20).

23. *Ad Gentes* (December 7, 1965), in *Documents*, pp. 584-630. See Roger D. Haight, "Mission: The Symbol for Understanding the Church Today," *Theological Studies* 37 (1976) 620-649, p. 633.

24. R. D. Haight, *art. cit.*, p. 632.

25. See Peter Chirico, "Dynamics of Change in the Church's Self-Understanding," *Theological Studies* 39 (1978) 55-75.

26. See R. P. McBrien, *op. cit.*, pp. 691-724.

27. The church is "... 'event'. The Church is, so to speak, a matter of 'continuous creation', produced by faith and charity, expressed above all in the sacraments." P. Fransen, *art. cit.*, p. 321.

28. John Henry Newman, *An Essay in the Development of Dogma* (London: Toovey, 1905), p. 39.

29. *Cum autem Ecclesia sit in Christo veluti sacramentum et instrumentum intimae cum Deo unionis totiusque generis humani unitatis. Lumen Gentium*, 1, in *Documents*, p. 15. As is well known, the use of the conjunction *veluti* reflects a compromise between the "liberal" and the more "conservative" positions of the Council Fathers.

30. See K. Rahner, *The Church and the Sacraments. Quaestiones Disputatae*, 9 (New York: Herder and Herder, 1967).

31. Cf. E. Schillebeeckx, *Christ the Sacrament of the Encounter with God* (New York: Sheed and Ward, 1963).

32. See R. P. McBrien, *op. cit.*, p. 716.

33. John Paul II, *Redemptor Hominis*, pars. 7, 19, 71, in *The Papal Encyclicals 1958-1981*, pp. 246, 250, 263.

# Chapter Three

## Theology and Experience

In a review of some of the salient developments in systematic theology in recent years, Richard McBrien began with the following observation: "If there is any insight which has become even more surely recognized in the last eight years, it is the recognition that the first theological question we ask ourselves is the question, 'Who am I?' 'Who are we?' It is precisely in our attempt to come to terms with the meaning of our own lives that we raise the questions of God, of Christ, and of the requirements of Christian existence."[1]

To this statement of his primary position, McBrien added the reflection that "Many Catholics have still not understood the fundamental principle that doctrine comes after, not before theology. Doctrines are themselves interpretations of the Church's experience of God."[2] This would seem to suggest that the primary locus for theological reflection ought to be neither the traditional symbols of the faith nor a specific theological tradition which has attempted to interpret the Christian experience of God (and still less ought the primary *locus* of theological reflection to be excerpted texts from Scripture, or, what is worse, an extended commentary on Denziger's *Enchiridion Symbolorum*).[3] Rather the primary locus of theological reflection ought to be the Christian experience itself, the experience of the church.[4]

In its *Decree on Priestly Formation*, Vatican Council II issued a challenge to base theology more directly on the lived experience of the church.[5] The preface (pars. 1-3) and the introductory statement (par. 4) of the Council's *Pastoral Constitution on the Church in the Modern World*,[6] clearly called for the church to read the signs of the times. Such scrutiny can hardly be considered as a take-it-or-leave-it activity of the church, as something quite optional. Rather, "the Church has always had the duty of scrutinizing the signs of the times and interpreting them in the light of the Gospel."[7] The reference, in a single stroke of the pen, to both the signs of the times and the light of the Gospel is a sure indication that the Fathers of Vatican II considered theology to be a dialogical endeavor.

## Tradition and Experience

That theology is to be elaborated in a dialogical
fashion is well illustrated in the works of the major
American theologians.  Commenting upon the works of such
giants as Orestes Brownson, John Ryan, and John Courtney
Murray, John A. Coleman has written that "Brownson,
Ryan, and Murray were each steeped in the full tradition
of Christian theology.  Each, however, moved beyond
theology to correlate his thought with a secular
discipline: philosophy, economics, and political science
respectively.  All three were significantly involved in
discerning the signs of their own times."[8]

It is not only the genius of these latter day
theologians which prompts us to opt for a dialogical
approach to theology.  Such was also the manner of
interpreting religious experience proper to Paul and
Aquinas.  It was the religious genius of Paul,
undoubtedly shaped and sharpened in the Damascus
experience, which moved him to bring the nascent
Christian tradition previously formed in a Judeo-
Christian matrix into relationship with the Hellenistic
world, where notions of the "Christ" and "the Son of
Man" were virtually incomprehensible.  It was the
lasting contribution of Aquinas to bring the
philosophical realism of Aristotle, as elucidated by
Arab thinkers, to bear upon a faith tradition mediated
through the centuries by Platonism and neo-Platonism.

In sum, some of the most influential of
theological thinkers have proceeded by allowing the
gospel message and a culture, a tradition and an
experience, not only to interface but also to interact.
Their approach should confirm the thesis that theology
is most profitably construed as being dialogical.

It is, however, one thing to affirm that theology
ought to be dialogical; it is another thing to allow the
dialogue to take place.  In a general sort of way, three
basic approaches to theology can be identified.[9]

The first approach is the classical theological
approach of Anselm and the neo-orthodoxy of Karl Barth.
This is the doctrinal approach to theology.  It attempts
to explain and offer a logical validation for the verbal
expressions of the faith.  It seeks to demonstrate the

rationality of the faith and interprets the "faith" of Anselm's famous definition of theology, "faith seeking understanding" (*fides quaerens intellectum*), as the faith which is believed, that is the formal, verbal, affirmations of faith throughout the centuries.

This doctrinal approach to theology is not without implications for conduct and life style. These are, however, best seen as corollaries to doctrinal elaboration or as applications to life of a doctrinal theory. For example, one might urge the reform of the rite of reconciliation on the basis of an historical study of the church's penitential discipline. As a matter of fact, it was the historical studies of Galtier,[10] Anciaux,[11] and others of their kind, which eventually led the Vatican II - inspired reform of the rite of reconciliation within Roman Catholicism. Yet the "reform" appears to have had little effect — most probably because it was not correlated with our experience.

A second major approach to theology is the method of correlation. This method is most commonly associated with the name of Paul Tillich.[12] It seems to be reflected in the work of such contemporary theologians as Paul Lehman,[13] Carl Peter,[14] and John Shea.[15] For Tillich the task of theology is, on the one hand, to formulate the questions implied in human existence, and, on the other hand, to formulate the answers implied by the divine self-manifestation in the light of the questions implied in human existence. In the Tillichian view of theology one responds to questions raised by the "situation" to answers offered by the "message". In a similar vein, Schubert Ogden speaks of the correlation of the Christian witness of faith and human existence.[16] There is an experiential, existential or ontic element in theology from the very outset. At bottom this approach to theology is also reflected in such Roman documents as *Gaudium et Spes* and *Lumen Gentium*.

A third approach to theology is the method of disputation. It is a method of doing theology which is found but rarely in the work of contemporary Roman Catholic thinkers[17] but is implicit in the approach to theology of many pators from among the various confessional groups within Christianity. As a formal approach to theology, it can be linked with the name of the Lutheran theologian Heinrich Ott.[18] Basically the method is both apologetic and existential. It implies that the meaning of a statement is to be discovered by seeking and acknowledging the conditions which would falsify it. In the doing of theology according to this mode, pastors preserve their integrity only by making their own the question implicit in circumstances or explicitly addressed, and answering it.

Each of these approaches to theology deals with the fact of the existence of the Christian (alternatively, the experience of the church) in its own fashion. Much has been written of late on theological method, explicitly in the works of Lonergan,[19] Walgrave,[20] Tracy,[21] O'Collins,[22] and implicitly in the theological summae penned by Macquarrie,[23] Ratzinger,[24] Rahner[25] and McBrien.[26] Running throughout these works is the basic notion that theology is dialogical.

David Tracy explained that "this commitment to determine methods and criteria which can show the adequacy of Christian self-understanding for all human existence is demanded by the very logic of the Christian affirmations; more precisely, by the Christian claim to provide the authentic way to understand our common human experience. This insight *theologically* disallows any attempt to force a strictly traditional inner-theological understanding of the sources of theological reflection. Whether that inner theological self-understanding be explicated through any of the forms of theological orthodoxy or through a kind of neo-orthodoxy represented by Karl Barth in the *Church Dogmatics* is a relatively minor matter. The major insight remains the insistence present in theological reflection at least since Schleiermacher: the task of a Christian theology intrinsically involves a commitment to investigate critically both the Christian faith in its several expressions and contemporary experience in its several cultural expressions."[27]

In his study of theological method, *Blessed Rage for Order*, Tracy has enunciated as the first of his five theses of a theological methodology that: "The two principal sources for theology are Christian texts and common human experience and language."[28] What Tracy has enunciated in this first thesis is, in fact, a commonplace in the history of systematic theology. Melchior Cano, a sixteenth century Spanish Dominican, was the first to develop a systematic presentation of the *loci theologici*, the sources for theological reflection. This was done in his famous work, *De locis theologicis libri duodecim*.[29] In this epoch-making work, Cano distinguished ten *loci theologici*. The first seven are: (1) Scripture; (2) the Tradition of Christ and the Apostles; (3) the Authority of the Catholic

Church; (4) the Councils, especially the General
Councils; (5) the Authority of the Roman Church; (6) the
Authority of the Fathers; (7) the Authority of
Scholastic Theologians. All seven of these sources for
theology belong to the category of "Christian texts",
albeit with differing degrees of authority and
normativity. Cano, however, did not limit his list to
these seven witnesses to the tradition of the church.
To the seven he added an additional three sources,
namely, (8) Natural Reason; (9) the philosophers and
jurists; and, (10) history (documentary and oral
tradition constituting and interpreting tradition). It
is not legitimate to infer from Cano's list of the
sources of theology that he had the same insights in the
sixteenth century as such moderns as Karl Rahner and
David Tracy have in the twentieth. To make such an
assertion would be to interpret Cano as a twentieth
century theologian with the consequences that he would
be as much out of step with his own times as was Hank
Morgan with King Arthur's Court. On the other hand, a
realistic study of Cano reveals that he looked beyond
the "texts" to "cultural" and "experiential" factors as
sources for theology.

Alternatively, we might choose to begin our
theological reflection with experience, instead of the
Christian tradition. We must, however, be wary of
speaking — whether in theological or other discussions
matters little — simply about "experience". We are not
passive recorders who contemplate our experience as an
external reality. We live our experience as conscious
and responsible human beings. Our "experience" is
always our experience such as we interpret it. A human
experience does not exist apart from the conscious
participation of those persons who are involved in it.
Human experience is always interpreted experience.[30]
Indeed the science of hermeneutics has always recognized
the problem of experience and its interpretation.[31] One
who would analyze experience[32] systematically and
scientifically must initially raise at least two
questions. What are the *tools* for interpreting
experience? What are the *criteria* for interpreting
experience? The Christian who would engage in
theological reflection would respond that although it is
legitimate and beneficial to interpret human experience
by means of the historical and behavioral sciences, it
is also legitimate, and even necessary (thus, his faith
conviction), to interpret human experience by means of
the Christian theological tradition.

With the notion that the two principal sources for theology are the Christian tradition and the human experience,[33] *datum et concessum,* one must ask how to move from one to the other. This is perhaps the basic question of theological methodology. David Tracy has summed up his own answer to the basic question by postulating as a second thesis that "the theological task will involve a critical correlation of the results of the investigations of the two sources of theology."[34]

The issue of the relationship between theological tradition and human experience is crucial for the minister who brings that theological tradition into the world of human experience. It is all the more crucial when the ministry includes a component of theological reflection. According to Laurence O'Connell, theological reflection is the "forum wherein the contemporary experience of the minister encounters the normative influence of tradition."[35] Conversely he has described theological reflection as the "process in which Christian tradition is brought into creative dialogue with contemporary experience."[36]

Spontaneously the minister asks, What is the relationship between doctrine and practice? Upon reflection, he or she becomes aware that this simple question implies another, What doctrine? The minister, if he or she reflects critically, should certainly be aware that there are different doctrinal systems which elicit different modes of practice.

The fully attentive minister should be no less aware that human experience is one of the traditionally acknowledged sources of "doctrine". Therefore the minister must reflect on the relationship between human experience and practice. How has human experience contributed to the formulation of a theological theory which elicits a given practice? How is the practice itself given concrete form in and by means of human experience.

### Ministry and Experience

This series of reflections and the questions to which they have led implies that theological reflection is no simple task. They have certainly warranted the conclusion that theological reflection is an important part of theological methodology and belongs to the discipline of fundamental theology. Yet theological

40

reflection can be examined, not only in its broadest generality, but also in a very concrete fashion. One can ask about the meaning of one's own ministerial experience, about the meaning of one's specific experience of church, that is, in the light of Christian texts and the common human experience. One can allow one's own experience to be the focus of the correlation between the results of the investigations of the Christian tradition and the common human experience. When one does so, one is doing an exercise — which ought to be an ongoing effort — in theological reflection as a ministerial task.

In other words, if the Christian tradition is one of the fundamental *loci* for theology, and if human experience is a fundamental *locus* for theology, then a concrete ministerial experience is a valid locus for doing theology (theological reflection). With respect to Christian tradition, it is presumed that a ministerial experience attests to the Christian tradition. It is a witness to and bearer of the Christian tradition. With respect to human experience, a given ministerial experience is not the common human experience (an abstraction, at best) but a specific human experience. Thus it is in the ministerial experience, that is in a concrete experience of the church, that Christian tradition and human experience meet in time and space.

In sum, theological reflection is an equivocal term. As a general process, it belongs to fundamental theology. As a process of reflection upon a concrete experience of Church, it is a pastoral skill, the theory of which is properly developed in ministerial theology. Yet all too often the basic question in ministerial theology is the seemingly simple question, how does one put one's doctrine into practice. I would suggest that it is equally legitimate to pose the question, how does one's practice reflect one's doctrine? Those who raise the first question could theorize about their activity in a manner which Karl Rahner has described as "practical theology", namely, "the scientific organization of the reflection upon the question how the Church's self-actualization is to take place out of and in response to its particular given situation in each instance."[37] Those who raise the second question can see their efforts in the light of a remark by Princeton's Seward Hiltner who wrote that "the context of pastoral theology is... the theological theory resulting from the study of the operation of pastor and church."[38]

In fact, one should ask not one or the other of
the questions raised in the preceding paragraph, as if
one had a choice. The minister must ask both questions.
If theology is essentially dialogical, neither theology
in general, nor ministerial theology in particular, can
opt for one approach over the other. It is not a matter
of either-or; it is a matter of both-and. Similarly,
Thomas F. McKenna has cited the "mutual priority" of the
ascending and descending movements at work.[39] In the
exercise of theological reflection as a ministerial
function, one might discern an emphasis on the movement
from theory to practice, or an emphasis upon the
movement from practice to theory, but the mutual
priority of both emphases must be asserted. It is only
when it respects this mutual priority that the
ministerial exercise of theological reflection is truly
theological, for it is only then that it involves the
critical correlation of the results of the scientific
investigation of the basic sources of theology.

That the exercise of theological reflection as a
ministerial skill is an endeavor which must be carried
out in dialogical fashion was strikingly emphasized by
James and Evelyn Whitehead who offered this description
of theological reflection: "By theological reflection we
mean the ability to bring the Christian tradition
(Scripture and our multi-level historical tradition)
into dialogue with our contemporary existence in such a
way as to yield both understanding of God's action in
the Church today and decisions about the building of
Christian community adequate to the future."[40]

Theological reflection is a dialogue; it must not
be a monologue. It is more than a matter of bringing
the insights of our theological tradition to bear upon
our experience. It is also to allow our experience to
enter into dialogue with and clarify some elements of
our religious tradition. The double movement of the
dialogue between tradition and experience was brought
out by the Whiteheads in their thoughts about the impact
of theological reflection on the one who participates in
it. "The student," they wrote, "learns how to allow his
experience to question his theological tradition as well
as how to allow the tradition to confront his
experience."[41]

The dialogical nature of theological reflection
was also emphasized in the *Program of Priestly
Formation*. In the first of their reflections upon the
nature of the pastoral skill of theological reflection,
the authors of the *Program* highlighted its dialogical

character as follows: "Theological reflection refers to that process by which they attempt to perceive how theology and the tradition of the Church shed light on various pastoral situations they have experienced, how God's saving power and presence are operative in these experiences, and what this means for their own life in Christ."[42]

Before attempting to develop a model(s) for theological reflection, it is of crucial importance to recognize the importance of the dialogical approach to theological reflection. One must look both to the theory which determines the practice, and to the practice which discloses the theory. In some senses the movement is circular because, as the philosopher Paul Ricoeur explains, "the symbol gives rise to thought; yet thought is informed by and returns to the symbol."[43] The reflection is pertinent to the task of theological reflection and the approach to theological reflection adopted in these pages. The church's activity, its ministry, essentially belongs to the category of symbol. It is the experience of those symbols which gives rise to critical reflection. This reflection, in turn, informs one's symbol-making and allows one to take responsibility for it.

We are, therefore, not really dealing with a circle when we are engaged in the process of theological reflection. If one critically analyzes the symbol one will find that it does not adequately reflect the doctrine from which it has emerged as a practical corollary. The gap thus discovered between the "rhetoric" (thought, doctrine) and the "reality" (the symbol, the ministry) will enable the analyzer to modify the symbol (the ministry). Thus the movement between doctrine and practice, if taken seriously and critically examined, will prove to be spiral, rather than simply circular. In essence this means that theological reflection is concerned with discerning the meaning of the symbols which one posits, the meaning of one's message, the meaning of one's ministry. To discern the meaning of one's ministry is what theological reflection is all about.

1.  R. P. McBrien, "Dogma," *Chicago Studies* 20 (1981) 137-150, p. 138.

2.  *Idem.*, pp. 143-144.

3.  See K. Rahner, "Reflections on Methodology and Theology," in *Theological Investigations*, 11, 68-114, pp. 70-71.

4.  See P. Fransen, *art. cit.*, p. 312, who writes, "The life of the Church, the *praxis ecclesiae*, embodies the faith of the Church in the course of history. This praxis is a *locus theologicus* for theological reflection." In a similar vein, Karl Rahner has written that "theology is only of interest when it constitutes a process of reflection (though obviously of course critical reflection) upon the faith of a Church which is actually using this faith as the basis of its activities." K. Rahner, "Reflections on Methodology," p. 81.

5.  *Optatam Totius*, pars. 13-21, in *Documents*, pp. 449-455.

6.  *Gaudium et Spes*, in *Documents*, pp. 199-203.

7.  *Gaudium et Spes*, 4 in *Documents*, p. 201.

8.  John A. Coleman, "Vision and Praxis in American Theology: Orestes Brownson, John A. Ryan, John Courtney Murray," *Theological Studies* 37 (1976) 3-40, p. 7.

9.  See William J. Close, "What Does It Mean to Think Theologically?", in *Theological Field Education. A Collection of Key Resources*, 2, ed. by Donald F. Beisswenger, Tjaard A. Hommes, and Doran McCarty (Kansas City: Association for Theological Field Education, 1979) 75-88, pp. 82-84. In *Blessed Rage for Order*, David Tracy has distinguished five basic models in contemporary theology: the orthodox, liberal, neo-orthodox, radical, and revisionist models. See David Tracy, *Blessed Rage for Order. The New Pluralism in Theology* (New York: Seabury, 1975), pp. 22-42.

10. Paul Galtier, *L'Église et la rémission des péchés aux premiers siècles. Bibliothèque de théologie historique* (Paris: Beauchesne, 1932).

11.  Paul Anciaux, *La théologie du sacrement de pénitence du XII^e siècle*. *Dissertationes ad gradum magistri in Facultate theologica... consequendum conscriptae*, II, 41 (Louvain: Nauwelaerts, 1949); *Le Sacrement de la pénitence. Etudes de théologie sacramentaire* (3rd ed., Louvain, Nauwelaerts, 1963).

12.  P. Tillich, *Systematic Theology*, 3 vols. (Chicago: University of Chicago, 1951-1964).

13.  Paul Lehman speaks of "contextual theology". See, for example, "On Doing Theology: A Contextual Possibility," in *Prospect for Theology. Essays in Honor of H. H. Farmer*, ed. by F. C. Headly (London: James Nisbet and Co.), pp. 134-135.

14.  See. for example, Carl Peter, "The Role of the Bible in Roman Catholic Theology, Part II," *Interpretation* 25 (1971) 87-94, esp. p. 87.

15.  J. Shea, "Introduction: Experience and Symbol, An Approach to Theologizing," *Chicago Studies* 19 (1980), 5-20.

16.  Schubert Ogden, "What Is Theology?", *Journal of Religion* 52 (1972) 22-40, p. 23.

17.  See, however, K. Rahner, "Reflections on Methodology," p. 71.

18.  See, for example, Heinrich Ott. *Das Reden vom Unsagbaren. Die Frage nach Gott in unserer Zeit* (Stuttgart: Kreuz, 1978).

19.  Bernard J. F. Lonergan, *Method in Theology* (London: Darton, Longman & Todd, 1971). In accordance with his cognitional theory, Lonergan's "transcendantal method" operates through levels of experience, understanding, judging, and deciding. On the importance of experience in Lonergan's theologizing, see Matthew Lamb, "Orthopraxis and Theological Method in Bernard Lonergan," in *Proceedings of the Thirty-Fifth Annual Convention, The Catholic Theological Society of America*, ed. by Luke Salm (New York: Catholic Theological Society of America, 1981) pp. 66-87. [N.B., The theme of the 1980 convention, whose papers are gathered in this volume, was "Christian Orthopraxis and the Emergence of New Meaning in Theology"]

20. Jan Hendrik Walgrave, *Unfolding Revelation. The Nature of Doctrinal Development* (London: Huthchinson, 1972). See further *Louvain Studies* 4 (1972-1973), pp. 3-12, "The Nature and Scope of Theology," pp. 245-254, "Changes in Christian Dogmatic Language," pp. 362-373, "History and Change in Theology".

21. David Tracy, *Blessed Rage for Order. The New Pluralism in Theology* (New York: Seabury, 1975). For a critical assessment of this work, see Avery Dulles, "Method in Fundamental Theology: Reflections on David Tracy's Blessed Rage for Order," *Theological Studies* 37 (1976) 304-316.

22. Gerald O'Collins, *Fundamental Theology* (New York: Paulist, 1981).

23. John Macquarrie, *Principles of Christian Theology* (London: SCM, 1966).

24. Joseph Ratzinger, *Introduction to Christianity* (London: Search, 1969).

25. Karl Rahner, *Foundations of Christian Faith. An Introduction to the Study of Christianity* (New York: Seabury, 1978). For an analysis of the importance of experience in the analysis of Karl Rahner, see Anne Carr, "Theology and Experience in the Thought of Karl Rahner," *Journal of Religion* 53 (1973) 359-376; Leo J. O'Donovan, "Orthopraxis and Theological Method in Karl Rahner," in *Proceedings of the Thirty-Fifth Annual Convention, The Catholic Theological Society of America,* pp. 47-65.

26. Richard P. McBrien, *Catholicism*, 2 vols. (Minneapolis: Winston, 1980).

27. David Tracy, *op. cit.*, pp. 44-45. The other theses are as follows: (2) The theological task will involve a critical correlation of the results of the investigations of the two sources of theology. (3) The principal method of investigation of the source "common human language" and "experience" can be described as a phenomenology of the "religious dimension" present in everyday and scientific experience and language. (4) The principal method of the investigation of the source "the Christian tradition" can be described as an historical and hermeneutical investigation of

classical Christian texts. (5) To determine the
truth-status of the results of one's investigation
into the meaning of both common human experience
and Christian texts, the theologian should employ
an explicitly transcendental or metaphysical mode
of reflection.

28. *Idem.*, p. 43.

29. Salamanca, 1563.

30. In this respect there is a certain similarity
    between experience and history. History is always
    an interpretation of the facts; analogously our
    experience is experience such as we personally
    interpret it. In the intrepretation of one's
    experience elements from the sociology of
    knowledge must certainly be taken into
    consideration. See Peter L. Berger — Thomas
    Luckmann, *The Social Construction of Reality. A
    Treatise in the Sociology of Knowledge* (Garden
    City: Doubleday, 1966).

    The Whitehead's have suggested that "It is
    useful to distinguish the information present in
    the minister's own experience and that information
    which arises more explicitly in the symbols, mores,
    and sciences of a culture. In the intrepretation
    of the cultural component, they suggest that
    attention be paid to: (1) past philosophical
    understandings; (2) political intrepretations of
    human community; (3) the social sciences; and
    (4) other religious traditions. See J. D.
    Whitehead — E. E. Whitehead, *op. cit.*, pp. 19-20.

31. See J. Christiaan Beker, "Reflections on Biblical
    Theology," *Interpretation* 24 (1970) 303-320, p. 312.

32. The Whiteheads have called attention to the
    ambivalence of Christian ministerial experience in
    these terms: "Reflection in pastoral theology
    begins with experience as already, in part,
    religious and Christian." See J. D. Whitehead
    E. E. Whitehead, *op. cit.*, p. 65, n. 3.

33. In his "third thesis", Tracy maintains that: "The
    principle method of investigation of the source
    'common human experience and language' can be
    described as a phenomenology of the 'religious
    dimension present in everyday and scientific
    experience and language." See D. Tracy, *op. cit.*,

pp. 47-48.

34. D. Tracy, *op. cit.*, p. 45.

35. Laurence O'Connell, "Theological Reflection and Ministerial Identity," in *Theological Field Education*, 165-169, p. 165.

36. *Idem.*, p. 166.

37. K. Rahner, "Practical Theology within the Totality of the Theological Disciplines," in *Theological Investigations*, 9 (New York: Herder and Herder, 1972) 101-114, p. 103.

38. Seward Hiltner, *Preface to Pastoral Theology* (New York: Abingdon, 1958), p. 69.

39. See Thomas F. McKenna, "Academic or Pastoral Theology: A False Dilemma," *The Priest* 34 (1978) 10-14, p. 12.

40. James D. Whitehead — Evelyn E. Whitehead, "Educational Models in Field Education," *Theological Education* 11 (1975) p. 273.

41. *Ibid.*, p. 277.

42. *Program of Priestly Formation* (3rd ed.) par. 197, p. 55.

43. Paul Ricoeur, "The Symbol Gives Rise to Thought," in *The Symbolism of Evil* (Boston: Beacon, 1967) 347-358.

Chapter Four

Non-Verbal Communication and

Theological Reflection

    To illustrate how symbol conveys a message which is not always adequate to the thought (doctrine) that one intends to express, some ideas popularized by Julius Fast's *Body Language*[1] might be helpful. For Fast, the science of kinesics studies body language, that is "any non-reflexive or reflexive movement of a part, or all of the body, used by a person to communicate an emotional message to the outside world."[2] Through one's bodily movements one conveys a message which may be independent of, which may confirm, or which may be at odds with what one actually says. While one may say "I am glad to see you", the speaker's glance at his watch may reveal that the greeting is rather superficial, whereas the pouring of a drink would be a confirmation of his verbal message.

    Through our bodies and our bodily actions we convey a message. The bodily message is inarticulate, but often highly expressive. It is very important to appreciate the significance of the bodily message because it is a significant part of one's total communication with another. Reflection on and discussion of the meaning of this "body language" can help one understand the real message that is being communicated. Fast explained: "A discussion of the signals sent and the signals received might enable a person to gain new insights. What messages do you send? Does your walk express the way you really feel, the way you think, you feel, or the way others see you? We send out certain signals of body language and it is possible to learn more about ourselves by listening to others interpret the signals that we send."[3]

    Ordinary human experience confirms the fact that it is not only by what one says that one "speaks" a message; one's posture and one's conduct are highly expressive. How often has each one of us not perceived the joy or the sorrow of another before the other even opened his or her mouth? The message which is conveyed through one's posture and behaviour, is as much a product of one's culture as is the language which one speaks. Just as it is necessary to understand a language (English, French, German) in order to understand what another is saying, it is necessary to interpret another's body language within the cultural conditions[4] within which this language is spoken.

I remember vividly my embarrassment when I was first invited to the home of a Belgian friend for dinner. In keeping with local custom I brought a small gift. Since flowers, wine or candy are considered to be the acceptable gifts for such an occasion, I purchased a dozen red roses to bring to my friend and his family. Greeted at the door, I presented the roses to my friend's wife whose facial color imitated the hue of the roses which she was holding. It was easy for me to perceive her embarrassment, even though we did not speak a common language. Later I discovered the cause of her embarrassment. In Belgium, red roses are the gift which a lover brings to his beloved.

This simple experience, never to be repeated by me, highlights the importance of body language. On the one hand, my offering of a gift was "body language" but it conveyed the wrong message, because I was poorly attuned to the cultural conditions in which my attempt to convey a message was being expressed. On the other hand, the embarrassment written on the face of my friend's wife conveyed a universal message that I could not misinterpret. That I was able to do so was a first step in my learning something about the cultural significance of my well-intentioned gesture. Through experience I learned the truth of Fast's reflection that: "Different cultures have different customs, and, of course, different body language. They also have different looks and different meanings to the same looks."[5]

What Fast tried to explain in his popular little book is otherwise expressed in communication theory and linguistic analysis. For George H. Mead, gesture is "the primary phenomenon out of which language in the full human sense emerges."[6] "The medium is the message" is a slogan for which the late Marshall McLuhan was justly famous. At the very least it underscores the reality that it is not the verbal content of the message that makes the greatest impact; rather it is the "package" in which it comes. Moreover, we find that a number of students of semiotics make a distinction between the "spoken word" and the "speaking word". The spoken word is that which is told (or written) in so many words; the speaking word is what Fast has called body language — the posture, gesture, or action that conveys a message to those who perceive it.

## The Non-Verbal Expression of Faith

Now if any individual conveys a message through the medium of bodily conduct, it is to be expected that the conduct of the body of believers also conveys a message. To those outside the body of believers the meaning of the message is interpreted according to the categories of their own culture. Accordingly, during the sixties when I was engaged in campus ministry, I used to refer to the Sunday Eucharistic liturgy as a protest on behalf of God. Such an intrepretation of "the Mass" was hardly adequate to my own understanding of the Eucharistic liturgy, but the analogy conveyed a meaning to those who did not share my rather sophisticated theological view of the sacramental activity of the church; and the comparison was more than superficially accurate.

In short, what the church does through its ministers[7] should be seen as an expression of its message. What the body of believers does, serves as an indicator of its faith, perhaps as much as what it says, perhaps even more than the creed which it professes with its lips. Indeed the history of the church amply attests to the fact that the church's conduct is expressive of its faith. In the patristic era, attention was paid to *orthopraxis* (correct conduct) as well as to orthodoxy.[8] The theological adage *fides et mores* has been in vogue since the time of Augustine. For centuries it referred to the "faith" and "customs" of the church, the latter being understood as an expression of faith alongside the traditional symbols of faith (the creeds).[9] In the medieval era, theologians universally acknowledged that a doctrine did not reflect the authentic teaching of the church unless it was "received" by the faithful. This medieval teaching on the "reception" of doctrine[10] indicated that the ancient scholastics were well aware that the lived response of the body of believers to a doctrine was an indication of its authenticity or lack thereof.[11] As Roman Catholicism's classic systematic theology developed its teaching on the sources of theology, it spoke of the liturgy as a *fons theologiae*. Liturgy was considered to be a "proper source" (*fons proprium*) for theology insofar as it was a witness to the constitutive tradition of the church.[12] In short, while modern

51

theologians may be calling attention to the experience of the church as a source for theological reflection,[13] the emphasis on experience as a primary witness to what the church believes is as old as theological reflection itself.

The minister who takes seriously the experience of the church, and his own ministerial experience, is engaged in a process which is consistent with the church's self-awareness throughout the ages. Because of the dialogical nature of theological reflection, he or she will find the method of correlation more suitable as a methodological approach to theological work than either the doctrinal or disputational approach. Through the use of the dialogical method of theology the minister will find that he or she is participating in ministerial activity at a different level of consciousness from that of mere experience. Using the dialogical method, the minister can understand and eventually make a judgement about the ministerial endeavors in which he or she is involved.

## Responsibility for the Future of the Church

To the extent that the minister consciously participates in ministerial activity at all three levels of consciousness, the minister is able to assume greater responsibility for his or her activity. The minister who wishes to assume responsibility for the church (or some sector of the church) cannot afford to let reflection consist simply in analysis and judgment. The ministerial person must make a decision. The making of decisions by the church's ministers is imperative because, in the words of David Tracy, the "present need becomes that of finding symbolic language which can allow the disclosure of the Christian God to 'happen' for the present actual situation."[14]

Adequately considered, therefore, theological reflection involves a "projection into the future from a reflection upon past experience". Theological reflection is hardly static. It is a dynamic activity which implies an openness to the future and a willingness to take responsibility for the future. In sum, the temporal co-ordinates of theological reflection are the past, the present, and the future. Theological reflection is a process whereby the Christian tradition of the past and the contemporary human experience are used to elucidate the meaning of the present ministerial situation in order that the minister might take responsibility for his or her future ministry and assume thereby some responsibility for the church's mission. A responsible openness to the future is, after its dialogical nature, the chief characteristic of theological reflection.

There are, to be sure, two different ways in which the minister can look to the future of the church. On the one hand, the minister can consider that the future of the church is shaped by human factors. He will speak of pastoral planning and decision-making. Her ministry will be action-oriented, and she will use a "growth-model" to analyze and interpret her activity. On the other hand, the minister can maintain that the future of the church results from divine activity. He can speak of the eschatological kingdom of God which is already but not yet. She will speak of the power of God ever creating the church anew. As a paradigm for reflection on the growth of the church, one could use the Markan growth parables.[15] In fact, neither approach is to be adopted to the exclusion of the other. The church is a divino-human reality. It is both institution and mystery. Since grace builds on nature, the minister must both work for the coming of the Kingdom and pray for the coming of the Kingdom.

Although many Christians are reluctant to look upon the church as sinful because of Lutheranism's popularization of the *ecclesia semper reformanda* slogan, it should be clear to all that sin permeates the church in its present condition, in its individual members, in its ministers, and in its institutions. The liturgy itself brings the sinfulness of the church to a very clear expression insofar as the normative Eucharistic celebration begins with a penitential rite. As the church celebrates its most solemn ritual, as it begins to involve itself in its most characteristic activity, it acknowledges its own sinfulness. In the first Eucharistic prayer Roman Catholics pray "though we are sinners, we trust in your mercy and love." The Fourth Eucharistic prayer affirms the sinfulness of the church as it makes the Christological affirmation that He is "like us in all things but sin". Thus when the Eucharistic liturgy is used as a source for theology, one is necessarily drawn to the conclusion that the church which celebrates the liturgy is a sinful church.

Seen from this perspective, the judgement and decision-making aspects of theological reflection are essential to an ecclesial *metanoia*.

To look upon theological reflection as a function of ecclesial *metanoia* is one significant approach to the purpose and nature of theological reflection. Theological reflection is, as it were, the formulation of the church's judgment of conscience.[16] This is quite accurate and not to be neglected as one elaborates a theory of theological reflection.

Yet one must not be one-sided in approaching theological reflection. John Leith has written that "theology is an art as well as a technique."[17] His statement is no less true of theological reflection. Tunnel vision and one-way streets must be avoided since theological reflection seeks to interpret ministerial practice in its broadest context. In this respect the point of view expressed by Thomas McKenna[18] is well worth noting. McKenna suggested that the method of "practical theology" involves the circular movement of five questions; (1) What should be? — the ideal (doctrine). (2) What is? — reality. (3) What can be? — theological politics, ecclesial politics (the art of the possible). (4) What will be? — decision. (5) What can be learned? — a learning process. He notes that the question with which one starts determines whether one is to follow the ascending or descending order.

## The Nature and Purpose of Theological Reflection

These short reflections on the future orientation of the theological reflection process reiterate the significance of a point stressed in chapter two, namely that theological reflection presupposes a definite ecclesiology. It must also be said that theological reflection presupposes a definite epistemology or theory of knowledge, as has already been suggested, as well as a definite anthropology (understanding of the human being). The operative anthropology of the present approach to theological reflection is one which affirms that the human person is a historically and culturally conditioned individual, who is nonetheless a free and responsible agent of change.

Within this perspective, and taking a clue from Tracy's assessment of the present needs of the church, one can say that theological reflection is a matter of understanding the meaning of ministerial activity, and of articulating that meaning, in order that the minister can take responsibility for his or her ministry.

Theological reflection is an activity which is theological in its methodology and theological in its intent. That theological reflection employs a useful, and perhaps necessary theological methodology, has been the principal theme of the present chapter. Now it must be affirmed that theological reflection is theological in its very purpose.

When westerns think of theology, *theou logia* (words of/about God), they normally think of a doctrine or theory of God. This understanding of theology derives from a philosophical understanding of theology. Theology has a rational content: it consists of comprehensible words about God. Many of the Fathers of the church had, however, a different understanding of *theologia*. They understood "theology" in the deepest sense of the Greek term, that is a hymn or glorification of God.[19]

If the Psalmist[20] and the Canticler[21] invite inanimate creation to bless the Lord, "Bless the Lord all you works of the Lord... Bless the Lord, you Heavens," what the ministers of the church do as an expression of their faith should also bless the Lord.[22] Their ministerial activity ought to sing the praises of the Lord. Theological reflection is an activity in which the minister of the church becomes involved in order that his ministry be *theologia* in this ancient and most radical sense.

In *Christ, the Sacrament of the Encounter with God*, Edward Schillebeeckx[23] developed the idea that the activity of the incarnate Jesus was at one and the same time the revelation of God to men and a response to God. At once it was on behalf of men and on behalf of God. Simultaneously it was liturgy and revelation. The same two-fold orientation is, by analogy and extension, characteristic of Christian ministry.[24] It is turned to God and turned to his people at one and the same time. The minister should look upon ministerial activity as a "speaking word" which simultaneously speaks God's praises and His revelation.

Ultimately, therefore, theological reflection has an enabling function. Its purpose is that ministerial activity be *theologia*, a speaking word, which hymns praise and thanksgiving to God even as it speaks to people about God. If ministerial activity is to be *theologia* in this double sense, the minister can hardly forego theological reflection. Theological reflection is a use of spoken words which allows ministerial activity to be a speaking word, *theologia* in the fullest and most radical sense of the term.

1. Julius Fast, *Body Language* (New York: M. Evans and Co., 1970). Reprinted: New York, Pocket Books, 1971. References will be to this reprint. A more philosophical approach to the importance of the body as the situs of meaning has been developed by the French philosopher Maurice Merleau-Ponty. See, for example, his *Phenomenology of Perception* (London: Routledge & Kegan Paul, 1962), especially "The Body as Expression and Speech," pp. 174-199.

2. J. Fast, *op. cit.*, p. 2.

3. *Idem.*, p. 78.

4. *Idem.*, pp. 136-139.

5. *Idem.*, p. 138.

6. G. H. Mead, *Mind, Self, and Society. From the Standpoint of a Social Behaviorist* (Chicago: Univeristy of Chicago Press, 1934).

7. Piet Fransen has written that "the life of the Church, the *praxis ecclesiae*, embodies the faith of the Church in the course of history." See, P. Fransen, "Orders and Ordination," in *Sacramentum Mundi*, 4, 305-327, p. 312.

8. Gerald O'Collins adds a third element to the classical pair, *orthoelpis*, i.e. confidence in the certain fulfillment of hope. See, "Experiencing the Divine Self-Commitment in Faith," in *Fundamental Theology*, pp. 130-156.

9. See Piet Fransen, "A Short History of the Meaning of the Formula *Fides et Mores*," *Louvain Studies* 7 (1978-1979) 270-301.

10. See Yves Congar, "La 'Réception' comme réalité ecclésiologique," *Revue des sciences philosophiques et théologiques* 56 (1972) 369-403.

11. See P. Fransen, "The Essence of Authority in the Church Today: Its Concrete Forms," *Louvain Studies* 9 (1982-1983) 3-25.

12. As a "proper source" of theology, the liturgy was distinguished from such auxiliary sources (*loci adiuncti*) as philosophy, history and law. See M. Nicolau-J Salaverri, *Sacrae Theologiae Summa* (Madrid: Biblioteca de Autores Christianos, 1950),

pp. 20-22.

13. "Theology is only of interest when it constitutes a process of reflection (though obviously of course critical reflection) upon the faith of a Church which is actually using this faith as the basis of its activities" writes Karl Rahner in "Reflections on Methodology and Theology," in *Theological Investigations* 11, 68-164, p. 80.

14. D. Tracy, *op. cit.*, p. 189.

15. The Seed Growing Secretly, Mark 4:26-29; The Mustard Seed, Mark 4:30-32.

16. Somewhat analogously, Rahner has written that practical theology is "the critical conscience of the other theological disciplines." See "The New Claims," p. 134.

17. John H. Leith, "The Bible and Theology," *Interpretation* 30 (1976) 227-241, p. 241.

18. See T. F. McKenna, *art. cit.*, p. 12.

19. Cf., L. J. O'Connell, *art. cit.*, p. 166; Frank Whaling, "The Development of the Word 'Theology'," *Scottish Journal of Theology* 34 (1981) 289-312, p. 297.

20. Ps 148. Cf. Ps 103:22; 145:10.

21. See Dan 3:52-90 (LXX).

22. See the Hymn for Midday Prayer:
    *Help us, O Lord, to live*
    *The faith which we proclaim,*
    *That all our thoughts and words and deeds*
    *May glorify Your Name.*
    (*The Liturgy of the Hours. According to the Roman Rite*, New York: Catholic Book Publishing Co., 1955).

23. E. Schillebeeckx, *Christ, the Sacrament of Encounter with God* (New York: Sheed and Ward, 1963).

24. This double orientation is present in the traditional notion that the minister is *pontifex*, a bridge-builder.

Chapter Five


The Search for a Model


In his reflections upon theological method,
Bernard Lonergan defined, albeit in preliminary fashion,
method as "a normative pattern of recurrent and related
operations yielding cumulative and progressive results."[1]
If theological reflection is to serve the several
purposes which have thus far been intimated, it would
seem that it is the more likely to be successful if some
method of theological reflection is developed. Given
the dialogical nature of theological reflection in
general, and the varieties of ministerial experience in
which the minister can be engaged, it would seem that a
method of theological reflection will be the more useful
to the extent that it can integrate various dimensions
of the reflection process.

Since the experience whose meaning is to be
elucidated is a multifaceted experience, which bears
similarities with a variety of other experiences in
life, it might be appropriate to look for a model or
models as we attempt to develop a method of theological
reflection.[2] Models of the disclosure type do not
attempt to picture the reality which they help to
clarify; rather, they help to disclose or re-present the
reality which they help to interpret by offering
significant analogies. Consequently a number of
contemporary theologians have found the use of a
model(s) a useful approach in the quest for the
interpretation of theological realities.[3]


*Semiotics, or the Interpretation of Signs*

Given the fact that the church's ministerial
activity is largely symbolic, belonging therefore to the
categories of "gesture" and "speaking word", it is
useful to seek a model for disclosing the meaning of
ministerial activity in the world of communications
theory and linguistic analysis. Semiotics is the
science which studies how signs signify, how signs
communicate meaning. Semiosis is the process in which
something functions as a sign. This process is
frequently analyzed by means of the information theory

triangle (ITT).

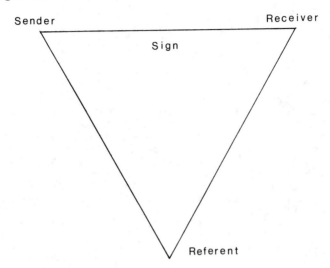

Sender                  Receiver

Sign

Referent

     This model sets out in schematic form the binary relationships of the components of the communications act, that is the sender and the receiver, the sign and its referent. The triangle offers a representation which suggests that the sign provides an almost physical connection between the sender and the receiver, and that a conceptual connection exists between the referent and all other components of the communication.[4]

     The spoken word belongs to the category of sign. Once a word or sentence is spoken and heard, the quasi-physical relationship between the sender and the receiver is established. Without such a relationship the communication is non-existent. Such would be the case when the intended receiver does not hear the message which is being addressed to him or her by the sender. This quasi-physical relationship is indicated by a solid line in the preceding diagram. The line can be identified as the pragmatic axis; that to which it refers is the quasi-physical relationship. One ordinarily uses the verb to "express" to indicate the process by which one articulates a message (sign) for the benefit of another (the receiver). We can use the verb to "impress" to indicate the process by which the other (the receiver) receives the message.[5]

     However there is more to the process of communication than the physical composition of sign.

A sign is a sign only when it actually signifies. For this it must not only make an impression, it must also have a meaning. It belongs to semantics to study the relationship between the sign and that which it signifies. Accordingly, the relationship between the sign and its referent might be identified as the semantic axis. In communications theory the referent is oftentimes called the *designatum*. When the referent is a concrete, extant reality it is often called the *denotatum*. Hence the verbs to "designate" and to "denote" are used to identify relationships along the semantic axis.[6]

Ordinary human experience confirms the importance of the perception of the relationship along the semantic axis for effective communication. Each one of us has had the experience of expressing a message with what we thought was crystal clarity, only to find out that our message was misconstrued by those upon whom it had made its "impression". Indeed it is the goal of effective speech to communicate the message which the speaker wants to communicate by words which are apt to convey the real meaning of the speaker's message to his receivers. For reasons far too numerous and too complex to warrant inclusion in the present pages, the relationship between the sign and the referent is often perceived in different ways by the sender and the receiver. Both sender and receiver are interpreters of the sign (see diagram on the following page). For this reason, people often suggest that the receiver of a message repeat the message before communication is broken off. The request for the repetition of the message is a simple check to assure that the relationship along the semantic axis of the communication has not broken down.

Ordinary human experience suggests that failure to communicate effectively often stems from yet another source. Parents, for example, frequently discover that their children do not respond obediently when commands are given. "I told you to... "., they say. A child, however, often says, "I didn't think that you really meant it." Children frequently think that parents are not serious about their commands because disobedience is not sanctioned. As a result they get the impression that certain types of commands are not worth the bother of being obeyed. Parents (and teachers) soon learn that consistency is necessary if communication is to be effective.

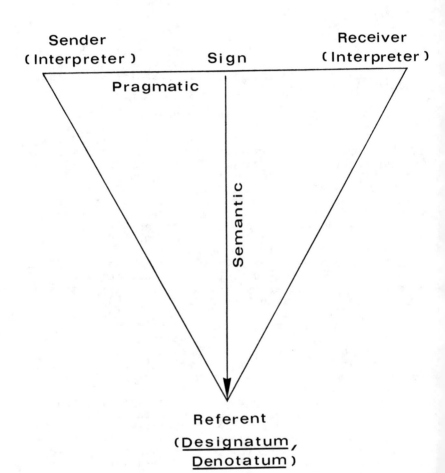

This common experience indicates that the context in which a message is conveyed is also an important element of effective communication. The age-old story about the boy who cried "Fire!! Fire!!" in the theater well illustrates the point. On several occasions, he had cried "Fire!". The patrons responded by leaving the theater while the performance was interrupted. But there was no fire. Angrily they returned to their seats. After this scenario had been repeated on several occasions, the patrons began to neglect the young boy's cries. Then one day there was a fire in the theater. The young boy cried "Fire!" but no one responded. The history of his previous conduct was enough to deprive his "message" of its ability to convey meaning.

Linguistic analysis draws attention to the linguistic context in which a message is communicating by speaking of the systems of signs to which a given sign belongs. When dealing with the sign of a written or spoken word the language (English, French, etc.) in which the message is expressed is an essential part of the sign system. Yet the signs system cannot be reduced to the collection of the words which comprise a language. When a message is communicated orally, the tone of voice and the accompanying gestures are also a part of the signs systems to which the spoken message belongs.[7]

Charles Morris[8] has therefore added a third axis to the ITT. This axis is the syntactic axis. It highlights the relationship between a sign and the other signs in the message. Pertinent to the relationship between a sign and the other signs in the sign system is the verb to "imply". Thus we have an expanded form of the ITT as follows:

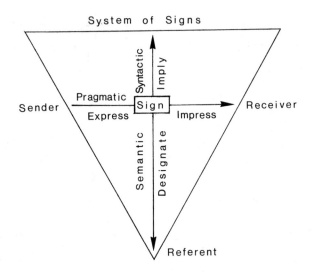

It should be clear that the process by which a sign signifies, that to which the triangle points, is a single process. All five correlates (the sender, the receiver, the referent, the sign system, and the sign itself) must be involved if the sign is to convey meaning. The three relationships, indicated by the pragmatic, semantic, and syntactic axes, may be abstracted and isolated for purposes of analysis, but they are aspects of one single process.

The science of semiotics studies how a sign conveys meaning. But there exists some confusion as to the "meaning of 'meaning'". Initially one might consider that meaning refers to the relationship between a sign and that which it signifies (the referent). However one occasionally speaks of "meaning" in the sense of importance or value. In somewhat related fashion, one might speak of the meaning conveyed to the receiver. Accordingly we sometimes say that a sign is meaningful in relationship to a receiver but as having meaning in relationship to its referent.

Semiotics does not claim that there is only one meaning of a given sign. Accordingly it would rather not say that a sign has meaning; instead it would hold that a sign is meaningful. Indeed, ordinary human experience indicates that signs are meaningful at different levels and in different ways according to the receivers who receive the sign. Scholastic philosophy was fond of citing the ancient adage, *quidquid recipitur in modo recipientis recipitur* (whatever is received is received according to the manner of the recipient). This is certainly true of signs. For a youngster who hears the message, "The Dodgers won the 1981 World Series" the message is meaningful. The same (physical) message is otherwise meaningful for an older person who understands the message in terms of the economic ramifications or the history of the traditional rivalry between the Dodgers and the Yankees. That a single message can have different meanings can be indicated by means of the technical term, polysemy.

Morris has also drawn attention to another point that may prove useful for our purposes. He has written that "signs normally take the place of objects they designate only to a limited extent, but if for various reasons interest cannot be satisfied in the object themselves, the signs come more and more to take the place of the object."[9] Some fusion of sign and object can be noted in the aesthetic field, but "the interpreter does not actually confuse the sign with the object it designates: the described or painted man is called a man, to be sure, but with more or less clear recognition of the sign status — it is only a painted or described man."[10] To some extent some fusion is seen in the economic field when a dollar bill is identified with wealth. More often a fusion between the sign and its object is experienced in the religious field. Thus, reflecting on some recent developments in Christology, John O'Grady commented that, "the great danger is that with the emphasis on the human as the expression of the divine the signified can be lost in the sign."[11] In Roman Catholicism, prior to the Second Vatican Council, the church (as sign) was often confused with the Kingdom of God (the "object"). Whenever fusion between the sign and its object occurs, some major difficulty arises from the mis-perception of the sign.

*Non-Verbal Signs*

The application of the ITT to an understanding of how a sign conveys its meaning has thus far been developed with regard to verbal signs. Most linguistic analysts study the verbal sign by preference. Indeed it is verbal signs which are the usual mode of precise communication among human beings. Yet verbal signs are not the sole mode of communication between humans, especially when one is communicating affect and emotion.

65

Gestures are an important form of communication between human beings. Mead's statement that the gesture is the "primary phenomenon out of which language in the full human sense emerges" is indeed apropos to the understanding of communication.

The importance of gestures in human communication is well illustrated in a short scene described in the Book of Esther:

"On the third day Esther put on her royal robes and stood in the inner court of the king's palace, opposite the king's hall. The king was sitting on his royal throne inside the palace opposite the entrance to the palace; and when the king saw Queen Esther standing in the court, she found favor in his sight and he held out to Esther the golden scepter that was in his hand. Then Esther approached and touched the top of the scepter. And the king said to her, 'What is your request? It shall be given you, even to the half of my kingdom.'[12]

In this little scene, Esther's attitude of waiting while appropriately adorned, the king's extension of the golden scepter, and Esther's touching the scepter are very significant gestures. The fact that Ahasuerus engaged Esther in dialogue is an indication that gestures often need to be followed up if they are to convey a message adequately.[13]

One must not draw from the fact that gesticular communication is often followed by oral communication the idea that gesticular communication is less expressive than oral communication. Indeed, in the game of baseball the base-runner receives his instructions from the coach almost exclusively in the manner of gesticular communication. Theater goers who have recently seen the British presentation of "St. Francis of Assisi" in mime and have given it rave reviews fully appreciate the power of gesture to communicate.

In many forms of human communication, however, gesticular communication and verbal communication are complementary to one another. In the words of Julius Fast, "body language and spoken language,... are dependent on each other. Spoken language alone will not give us the full meaning of what a person is saying, nor for that matter will body language alone give us the full meaning. If we listen only to the words when someone is talking, we may get as much of a distortion as we would if we listened only to the body language."[14]

Since the verbal and non-verbal "language" are complementary to one another, the sign system to which a message phrased in verbal language really belongs includes a quota of non-verbal signs. The stare and the smile are powerful companions of the spoken word. Even when a message is communicated by means of the written word, non-verbal factors often contribute to the meaning of the message. To illustrate the point, one need only reflect on how one might re-act to the telegram, airmail letter, surface mail, and third-class mail. The same (physical) message might be conveyed through any one of these four media, but the "message" varies somewhat according to the medium of communication.

On the other hand, the sign system to which a message conveyed non-verbally belongs often includes a quota of verbal signs. Typically the verbal signs interpret the non-verbal communication, oftentimes as a follow-up. This was the situation of Ahasuerus who interpreted the meaning of his gestures which he addressed to Esther. That gestures need to be interpreted if they are to serve as an effective means of communication is the experience of everyone who has had to explain his or her personal conduct to another. The need for interpreting gestures is also the experience of the church, which has added an interpretive word to the gestures performed in its sacramental rites.[15]

Of itself the gesture of pouring water can be the bearer of a variety of meanings. Water is poured to cleanse, to cool, and to slake thirst (and any combination thereof). It is the words which accompany the pouring and the context within which the water is poured that makes of the simple gesture of pouring water the sacrament of baptism. In effect the church has had to deal with the phenomenon of the ambiguity of gesticular signs. It recognizes that gestures are ambivalent and/or vague. By accompanying its sacramental gestures with words the church is implicitly recognizing the polysemy of the gesture-sign.

The ambiguity of word and gesture as means of communication (an aspect of the phenomenon of polysemy) as well as the fact that it is the total context (the entire sign system) which must be taken into consideration if the meaning of the "message" is to be understood is well illustrated in Jesus' Parable of the Two Sons:

"What do you think? A man had two sons; and he
went to the first and said, 'Son, go and work in the
vineyard today.' And he answered, 'I will not'; but
afterward he repented and went. And he went to the
second and said the same; and he answered, 'I go, sir,'
but did not go. Which of the two did the will of his
father?"[16]


## The Church's Significant Activity

This parable serves as a useful transition from
communication theory applied to verbal and non-verbal
signs to the activity of the church and the ministerial
activity of its ministers. Both what the church says
and what it does are forms of communication. Both what
the minister says and what he or she does are means of
communication. Teaching and activity belong to a single
"sign-system". Teaching and activity are complementary
to one another and are mutually interpretative.

That they are so has been the understanding of
churchmen throughout the ages, even if they were not
able to use the language of semiotics to express their
understanding. St. John of Capistrano (1386-1456), for
example, wrote: "As Gregory says, 'When a man's life is
frowned upon, it follows that his teaching will be
despised.'"[17] Indeed, in the very first words that he
wrote[18] Paul argued from the integrity of his conduct to
the authenticity of his message. The importance of the
church authenticating its teaching by its activity was
highlighted by the bishops who gathered at Rome for the
Third International Synod (1971). They proclaimed:
"While the Church is bound to give witness to justice,
she recognizes that anyone who ventures to speak to
people about justice must first be just in their eyes.
Hence we must undertake an examination of the modes of
acting and of the possessions and life styles found
within the Church itself."[19]

That action and teaching be seen as correlative
means of communication is extremely important for
understanding the reality of the ministerial activity in
which one is engaged. Attention to this correlation is
vitally urgent if indeed the church is to proclaim the
Gospel effectively. Roger Haight made the point
succinctly when he wrote that "a Church whose nature is
sign-bearing but which does not actually or actively
signify what it professes becomes by definition a
counter-sign."[20]

The church is indeed sign-bearing. It is symbolic by its very nature. It is a sort of living metaphor of the Kingdom of God. Its symbolic activity proceeds from faith (hope and love) and elicits faith, hope, and love. Hence some reflection on the way in which metaphor "communicates" can elucidate some aspects of the way in which the church communicates its message. Roger Hazelton has noted that "the merits of the metaphor are neither referential nor descriptive, but affective, participative, and as Max Black would say, interactive. It does not follow that they are on that account wholly or merely 'subjective' either."[21] The remark is indeed pertinent to the symbols of faith. Those who take seriously the fact that faith is expressed in symbolic fashion must consider that "the truth about metaphorical truth, therefore, is bound up with what any metaphor does and how it does it. 'Seeing through language' is its function, not using language to illustrate truth otherwise arrived at."[22]

Hence the church, through its ministers, must be engaged in the process of theological reflection. Its action and its teaching are mutually interpretive. What is the real message that is being communicated? Such is the question that fires the zeal of those engaged in theological reflection.

Another reflection by Roger Haight goes straight to the heart of the matter. "Working from the principle that action and understanding are mutually determinative," he wrote, "the theological question of the Church in today's world becomes a reciprocally related double question. What understanding of the Church is necessary to mediate her performance in the world, and what understanding is necessitated by the action that is demanded of the Church by the world?"[23]

While we can and must ask this double question of the church's performance in general,[24] the question must also be asked in such a way that it focuses in upon the church-related activity of each of its members. One must ask the meaning of various forms of ministerial — "pastoral", if the minister is a "pastor" — activity. Since the ministry embodies a message, one can ask what is the message that is being communicated by one's ministry. In sum, theological reflection considers pastoral or ministerial activity as a "message" and then asks "What is the meaning of the message?"

Technically, the one who asks this question is attempting to analyze the semiosis of that sign which is

ministerial activity. It will prove useful to use the
ITT as a model for analyzing ministerial activity. When
one begins to do so, one is immediately confronted by
the fact that the question "What is the meaning of the
message?" is not a simple one. One is dealing with the
"meaning effect" of one's activity upon various publics.
In short, the phenomenon of polysemy must be taken into
account when one asks about the meaning of ministry.

When one uses the ITT as a vehicle for analyzing
the meaning effect of one's ministry, one should take
into account the fact that the horizon of one's question
as well as the horizon of one's activity, is theology.
The God-reality is both the perspective from which one
engages in ministerial activity and the ultimate
horizon of one's theological reflection. One asks the
question of the meaning of one's message in order that
that message (one's ministry) might be more effectively
theological in the double sense previously explained.
The one who engages in theological reflection must
always take cognizance of the fact that God's
relationship with us humans, and our relationship with
him is a mediated relationship. The humanity of the
mediation can never be neglected.

### Some Examples

A few examples might indicate how the ITT can be
of value in analyzing ministerial activity.

### Example 1: A Meeting of the
### Parish Council

It is quite evident that "the parish council
meeting" is an abstraction. What should be subject to
analysis is a specific meeting, held at a definite time
and in a certain place with identifiable participants, a
specific agenda, and a given mode of operation. It is
this particular parish council meeting which is
significant (i.e. serves as a sign) to those who observe
it. Thus we have the following schema:

70

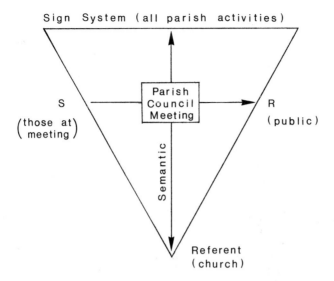

Sign System (all parish activities)

Parish Council Meeting

S

(those at meeting)

R

(public)

Semantic

Referent (church)

In the case of the parish council meeting, the senders of the "message" are those who participate in the meeting of the parish council. The message is being sent to parishioners, to wider church units, and to people who have no church affiliation at all. Presumably there is no great need to distinguish among these various recipients of the message since the polyvalence of a given parish council meeting is relatively low. Thus the recipients might simply be described as "the public".

As a sign the parish council meeting refers to the church. The fact that a meeting is held, in which the pastor (and other clergy?) and laity participate, is a sign of a populist vision of the church.

The agenda and mode of action would show just how consistent with the populist vision of the church the parish council meeting really is. Should the agenda be limited to temporalities, the message communicated by the parish council meeting is that the laity are truly responsible for the church only with respect to its institutional elements, and to a limited number of its institutional elements at that. The message communicated is that of a dichotomous church, in which institutional elements can be separated from the mysterious reality. This implies that matters of faith are the preserve of the pastor (or clergy) while financial responsibility is the lot of the laity.

Reflection along the syntactic axis will confirm whether or not this is, in fact, the case. Most often it does. The total "sign system" bears upon the participation of the laity in the life of the parish. How extensively and in what manner are they really involved in the life of the parish — its social activity, its liturgy, its charitable activity, its catechetical activity, etc.? More often the laity's real responsibility in various facets of church life will confirm one's interpretation of the relationship between a parish council meeting and a vision of the church as a referent.

Of course one could reflect that the agenda does not deal with matters of faith (liturgy, catechesis, and so forth) because the laity are not qualified to deal with these matters, even though they are otherwise involved in the life of the parish. They do function as lectors during the celebration of the liturgy, they are involved in various charitable and social activities, but they are not competent in matters of faith. Perhaps this is true. If it is, the one who engages in theological reflection must ask about the nature of faith. What is the meaning of the personal act of faith? Is it the responsibility of the clergy alone to communicate the faith? Why don't the laity have the possibility of expressing their faith in a faith-ful, and mature, fashion? It is questions such as these which arise from a simple act of reflection on a meeting of the parish council.

On the other hand, one might consider how the mode of action of the parish council designates the populist notion of the church. Elements of political analysis (perhaps even reflections on Robert's *Rules of Order*) will indicate how the meeting is actually conducted. Who has the power? How is it exercised? If the pastor has veto power and if he has used it in the past — in which case his exercise of the veto power would be part of the sign system — is a populist vision of the church really reflected by the meeting of the parish council? Indeed the autocratic or democratic posture of the pastor in other situations in which he has had to deal with parishioners would be part of the sign system implied by the specific parish council meeting under consideration.

To analyse a bit of pastoral activity in this fashion is not yet to find a solution for any of the problems, tensions, or inconsistencies which are brought to the surface in the analysis. The exercise is merely an exercise in understanding and judging so that one can take responsibility for one's activity.

Example 2: The baptism of the infant child

of cultural Catholics

Oftentimes the pastor of a parish is asked to celebrate the sacrament of baptism for a child whose parents are "cultural Catholics". These are individuals whose heritage is quite Catholic.[25] Most likely they would never deny their Catholic faith. Indeed, in some cases they are quite adamant in the affirmation of their Catholicity. However, they are not practicing Catholics. They are not involved in the life of the church. At most, they might appear for Easter and Christmas; at the least, they probably turn to the church on the occasion of birth, marriage, and death, perhaps first (or solemn) communion as well. Prudentially the pastor judges the infant to be brought to him will not be reared in the faith. At most the pastor might expect to see the child again at the time when it has reached the age for first communion. The baptism of the child is a sign, not only because it is a matter of the celebration of sacrament, traditionally understood within the category of sign, but also because it would be a communication to those who observe the baptism.[26] What is the real message which is conveyed?

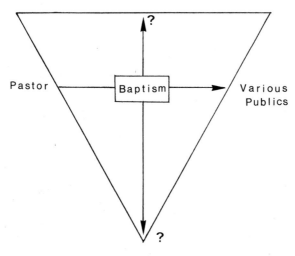

The sender of the sign would be the priest or
deacon who is to perform the ceremony. He allows his
theology to dictate the meaning of the sign along the
semantic axis. According to this interpretation, the
sacrament of baptism signifies adoption as a child of
God and incorporation into the church. In the pastor's
view, the rite is full of meaning. Thus:

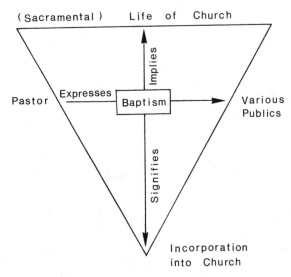

On the other hand, reality dictates that the
pastor consider the relationship between the celebration
of this sacrament and the child's involvement in the
life of the church. These are considerations to which
the syntactic axis points. If there is to be little or
no involvement in the life of the church the sacrament
hardly signifies incorporation into the church. The
intended celebrant might well reflect that if the
baptism will not "actually or actively signify what it
professes" it will become a counter-sign. His fear, a
legitimate one, is that the sacrament will be reduced to
some sort of a magical rite by which adoption by the
deity is "assured". If not that, he might reflect that
the realities implied by the syntactic axis are those
associated with birth into a family which has a specific
cultural heritage. As such, baptism is an important
event with tremendous cultural and social importance.
It would be on a par with enrollment in the local civil
registry, the wearing of the appropriate infants'
clothes, perhaps sleeping in the family's centuries old
cradle.

A reflection of this sort will certainly bring to the surface the inherent polysemy of the rite of infant baptism. It can be understood as a sacrament of the church, as a quasi-magical rite of adoption (or an "insurance policy" which will keep the child from damnation), or a traditional birth rite.

Should the baptism be celebrated, one might consider the various publics to whom a message is being communicated, and in this way come to a further appreciation of the phenomenon of polysemy, as it pertains to the baptism of an infant child of cultural Catholics. The receivers of the message are the parents and relatives, devoted members of the church, and neutral observers, to cite but three groups who would try to make sense of the celebration of the rite.

If the parents do not intend to rear the child in the faith, it would seem that they have an interpretation of the rite different from that had by the pastor. Perhaps they are interested in having the child's soul cleansed of sin so that it would not be condemned by an all-just God should it die in infancy. More positively they might think of baptism as a rite by means of which adoption as God's child is effected. On the other hand, they may be seeking the baptism of the infant simply because it is customary within their family that children be baptized. Then again it may be that they consider that baptism is a sacrament of incorporation into the church, but that their notion of church, based on their cultural and historical experience, does not require a very high degree of participation by its members.

From the parents' point of view, the realities along the syntactic axis belong to the category of care of the infant. It is the parents' love and care for the child that leads them to petition its baptism. Should the pastor then refuse to celebrate the baptism, the message which he communicates to the parents is that he does not care about their child. Having reduced the significance of the rite along the semantic axis (from "incorporation into the church" to "belonging to a Christian family"), the parents would interpret the pastor's refusal gesture along the syntactic axis which is the dominant element in the parents' understanding of the rite of baptism. Since the pastor is the symbol of the church, his refusal to baptize expresses to the parents (and their relatives) the church's disinterest in the infant.

Thus, for the parents:

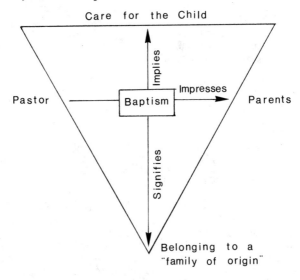

Care for the Child

Pastor → Baptism → Parents

Implies

Impresses

Signifies

Belonging to a
"family of origin"

The celebration of the baptism of the infant child
of cultural Catholics (or the refusal of baptism) will
make a different "impression" upon the members of the
church at large, even upon its devoted members,
according to their understanding of the sacrament of
baptism. To the extent that the sacrament of baptism
principally denotes the cleansing of the soul from
original sin and/or adoption as a child of God, they
would perceive the celebration of the rite as very
meaningful and would condemn the refusal to celebrate
the rite as a tremendous injustice to an infant child
who cannot provide for its own needs. To the extent
that baptism is seen principally as a sacrament of
initiation, the pastor's refusal to celebrate the
baptism of a child of merely "cultural Catholic" parents
would be consistent with a vision of the church which
points to personal involvement and commitment. How can
there really be an initiation, if there is to be no
follow-up? Alternatively, his celebration of the
sacrament would seem to make a mockery of what church
membership really means.

An outside observer who analyzes the total
semiotic process cannot help being confused. The priest
thinks that baptism means one thing; the parents think
baptism means something else. Priest and people are at
odds with one another. The church, which expresses

itself in the rite of baptism, is in a state of confusion. Yet the outside observer really need not be disturbed. Confusion as to infant baptism confirms what he or she has always thought — the church is really irrelevant. Should the priest baptize the infant, he is engaging the infant in a way of life which the parents judge to be irrelevant because they do not follow up the baptism with a life's involvement in church. Should the priest refuse to baptize the infant, he is demonstrably insensitive to a family's felt needs for its infant child. Who needs a church, so insensitive to the pulse of the human heart?

*Example 3: The church's teaching*

*on abortion*

The official teaching of the Roman Catholic Church on abortion is relatively clear. It has been verbally enunciated on many occasions throughout the ages. For instance, Vatican II's *Pastoral Constitution on the Church in the Modern World* stated: "From the moment of its conception life must be guarded with the greatest care, while abortion and infanticide are unspeakable crimes."[27] Similarly a November 13, 1973, resolution of the (United States) National Conference of Catholic Bishops clearly affirmed that "abortion, the destruction of a living human being in the womb of its mother, is morally wrong. No law or judicial opinion can change the moral judgement."[28]

Expressed verbally, this teaching belongs to the order of sign. The sender of the sign are the organs of the magisterium, and those who teach "in the name of the Church." Since the teaching speaks of the dignity, sanctity, or value of human life it is relatively easy to analyze the teaching activity of the church on the subject of abortion by means of the simple form of the ITT. The apexes are clearly identified: the magisterium and its organs, all human beings, and the value of human life. Thus:

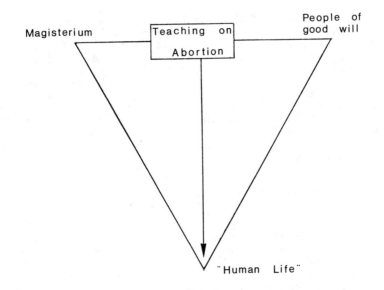

One can leave to the theologians and the
philosophers the discussion as to whether the teaching
of the church is adequate to the reality (the discussion
along the semantic axis). For the moment it can be
conceded that the traditional teaching, of and in
itself, is clear. However this teaching is always done
within a given context. When one analyzes the real
situation within which the church's teaching on abortion
is voiced, one begins to perceive some of the reluctance
on the part of many to accept this teaching. It is
expressed well, but doesn't make much of an impression.
Why not?

Because of the situation of the one upon whom the
teaching is being impressed. We cannot enter into a
lengthy discussion of contemporary anthropology at the
present time. Let it only be said that those who live
in the Western world are generally pragmatists, who have
a functional view of the world. This functional view of
the world represents, to a larger extent, an
unarticulated existentialism. What does this mean to
me? What value does that have for me? Of what use is
that to me? These are the types of questions that
represent the lay person's version of the philosopher's
existentialism. So the average western man or woman in
the street is both a pragmatist and an existentialist.

The pragmatist's world view certainly considers
that two are better than one. The impression that he

has of the church's teaching on abortion often derives from a presentation — one that I have heard myself — which emphasizes that even when the mother's life is endangered, and can be preserved only by means of an abortion, abortion is still to be rejected as morally wrong. Many, if not most, of our contemporaries cannot understand this because one life is surely of more value than no life at all. Isn't it preferable, they ask, to save the life of the mother at the expense of the life of the child, rather than lose both lives?

The existentialist's world view is such that he or she discerns the presence of personal life when there are signs of personhood. Personhood is realized to the extent that one interacts with other human beings. In adult life, dialogue is the form in which interpersonal communication normally takes place. In the life of the infant, anticipatory signs of this interpersonal interaction are readily perceived. The child's responsive smile, the fact that it dozes off into sleep when cuddled in the arms, the "coo", the crying, all these are so many forms of interpersonal communication. The existentialist would certainly hold that the relatively advanced process of interaction had by the infant child did not begin immediately at birth,[29] and thus would generally postulate the existence of personal life in the later stages of pregnancy. However the existentialist who understands truly human existence in terms of personhood and interpersonal interaction often finds it difficult to postulate personal existence of the fetus in the earliest stages of its existence.

This is not to suggest that the Church must change its teaching on the subject of abortion. It simply reflects the fact that the teaching frequently *does not make an impression* because those who are expressing the teaching have not sufficiently taken into account the real condition of the receiver to whom their teaching is being addressed.

From a consideration of the teaching on abortion along the pragmatic axis, we can turn to a consideration of the same teaching along the syntactic axis. Our earlier discussion and Morris' expanded ITT have shown that semiotics must be as attentive to the syntactic dimension as it is to the pragmatic aspects of the sign. In view of this, what is implied by the Church's teaching on abortion?

Another way of phrasing this question is, "what does the Church say about the value of human life?"

Here one encounters a fair amount of ambiguity. To a large extent the Church's witness on the value of life includes its teaching on war and peace. In recent years much has been made on the Just War Theory. It is a practical principle. War is justified provided that certain conditions are met.[30] One can easily draw the conclusion that human life is not an absolute moral value. Similarly, one can draw attention to the church's position on capital punishment. According to press reports, the traditional teaching which held that capital punishment was warranted in certain cases has been reiterated by John-Paul II.[31]

Thus the church does not seem to have a consistent statement on the value of human life. Of course one might object that in the current abortion discussion it is not "human life" as such but "innocent human life" which is the focus of the church's official concern. In this case, "innocent human life" is to be placed at the referent apex of the ITT. Then, in consideration of the syntactic axis, one would have to consider whether the church is consistent in its witness to the value of innocent human life. Indeed, in the light of the New Testament one would have to question whether "innocent human life" is a Gospel value.[32]

By way of a general conclusion to these considerations on the three examples, we should note, once again, that the process of conveying meaning, semiosis, is one single process. When one element is lacking the sign is not truly "meaningful". Reflections along the semantic axis raise questions of accuracy and clarity. Reflections along the syntactic axis raise questions of consistency and authenticity. In short, the ITT would seem to be a model, indeed almost a paradigm, for considering the meaning of ministry.

1. B. Lonergan, *Method in Theology*, p. 4.

2. The use of models has been taken over from the physical and social sciences where "the use of models is effective if the model allows for deductions as well as verification." Ramsey had noted that "in any scientific understanding a model is better, the more prolific it is in generating deductions which are then open to experimental verification and falsification." See Ian T. Ramsey, *Models and Mysteries* (New York: Oxford, 1964), p. 4.

   Writing of the possibility of a model to integrate various facets of a reality, John O'Grady has noted "when a model has successfully solved a great many questions and problems and allows for the greatest number of deductions and further invites a variety of personal understandings, then we have the meaning of a paradigm as expressed by T. Kuhn." Kuhn has described paradigms as "concrete puzzle-solutions which, employed as models or examples, can replace explicit rules as a basis for the solution of the remaining puzzles of normal science." See Thomas S. Kuhn, *The Structure of Scientific Revolutions* (Chicago: University Press, 1970), p. 176; John F. O'Grady, *Models of Jesus* (Garden City: Doubleday, 1981), pp. 26-27, 32, 35.

3. Among the innovators were Ian Ramsey (*Models and Mysteries*, New York, Oxford, 1964) and E. Cousins ("Models and the Future of Ministry," *Concilium*, 7 (1969), pp. 78-91). The use of models was popularized by Avery Dulles in *Models of the Church. A Critical Assessment of the Church and its Aspects* (New York: MacMillan, 1974).

4. See Susan Wittig, "Meaning and Modes of Significance: Toward a Semiotic of the Parable," Chapter VI in *Semiology and Parables. An Exploration of the Possibilities Offered by Structuralism for Exegesis, Pittsburgh Theological Monograph Series*, 9, ed. by Daniel Patte (Pittsburgh: Pickwick, 1976), 319-347, p. 321.

5. See Charles W. Morris, "Foundations of the Theory of Signs," in *Foundations of the Unity of Science*, 1, ed. by Otto Neurath, Rudolf Carnap, and Charles W. Morris (Chicago: University Press, 1961) 78-137, p.85.

6. *Ibid.*

7. See J. Fast, *op. cit.*, p. 108.

8. See C. W. Morris, *art. cit.*, p. 85.

9. *Idem.*, p. 120.

10. *Ibid.*

11. See J. F. O'Grady, *op. cit.*, p. 115.

12. Est 5:1-3.

13. See J. Fast, *op. cit.*, p. 23.

14. *Idem.*, p. 108.

15. The importance of the interpretive word was emphasized in traditional western sacramentology which spoke of the "matter" (the gesture) and "form" (the interpretive word) of the sacraments. The tradition goes back to Jesus himself (see 1 Cor 11: 23-25) and has its roots in the biblical tradition of the prophetic sign (*'oth*).

16. Matt 21:28-31a.

17. John of Capistrano, Mirror of the Clergy. Part I (Venice, 1580). Cited in *The Liturgy of the Hours According to the Roman Rite*, IV, p. 1508.

18. See 1 Thes 1:5; 2:9-12.

19. *Synod of Bishops, The Ministerial Priesthood, Justice in the World* (Washington: United States Catholic Conference, 1972) p. 44.

20. R. D. Haight, "Mission, the Symbol," p. 644.

21. Roger Hazelton, "Theological Analogy and Metaphor," *Semeia* 13 (1978) 155-176, p. 171.

22. *Idem.*, p. 174.

23. R. D. Haight, *art. cit.*, p. 637.

24. While theological reflection ought to be done with respect to the church as a whole, specific responsibility for the general task lies principally upon those who are especially charged with general responsibility within the church. Moreover, some theological reflection upon the

church as a whole is frequently found in the various works of ecclesiology. For each of these reasons, and others as well, we will forgo this general theological reflection within these pages.

25. In an article which treats of this very question, François Favreau has underscored the existence of "Christian remnants" in families which are no longer Christian. See F. Favreau, "La Demande du baptême: Que Veulent les Parents?", *La Maison-Dieu* 89 (1967) 87-100.

26. That is, not only those physically present at the celebration, but also those who "look at" the situation.

27. *Gaudium et Spes*, 51 in *Documents*, p. 256.

28. "Resolution of the National Conference of Catholic Bishops on the Pro-Life Constitutional Amendment. November 13, 1973," in *Documentation of the Right to Life and Abortion* (Washington: United States Catholic Conference, 1974), 45-46, p. 45.

29. This point of view, of course, is confirmed by various psychological studies.

30. In this respect, a certain analogy can be drawn between the evolution on the church's tradition on war and the evolution of the stand of secular society on abortion. Augustine and Thomas considered that war was something less than an ideal situation. To speak of war implied that charity, the norm, had failed. Later casuistry, however, developed the Just War Theory — in fact, an application of the principle of the Two-Fold effect. This Theory spoke of the justification of war, when the provisos were met.

    In Anglo-Saxon common law was considered as a crime, at least from the moment of quickening. Occasionally extenating circumstances that sanctions not be applied to the perpetrator of the crime. In the revision of the American Law Institute's Model Penal Code, however, the formulation was changed. "The termination of pregnancy is justified if... "

31. Econtra, "In 1974, out of a commitment to the value and dignity of human life, the Catholic bishops of the United States declared their opposition to

capital punishment." See *Community and Crime. A Statement of the Committee on Social Development and World Peace* (Washington: United States Catholic Conference, 1978) par. 44, p. 11.

32. See Mark 2:17; Gal 2:17, etc.

## Chapter Six

## The Value of Theological Reflection

Karl Rahner once wrote that "theology is only of interest when it constitutes a process of reflection (though obviously of course critical reflection) upon the faith of a church which is actually using this faith as the basis of its activities."[1]  Theological reflection makes theology "of interest".  This "interest" is due to the fact that theological reflection, a theologically legitimate endeavor, is pastorally necessary, and personally useful.

### *Theologically Legitimate*

Although the use of the ITT is of relatively recent origin, and although the ITT has, so far as can be determined, not hitherto been used as a vehicle for theological reflection, the legitimacy of theological reflection is amply indicated within our theological tradition.  One might begin with examples of theological reflection cited within the pages of the New Testament Scriptures.  Jesus made use of the notion of the Kingdom of God to reflect on the significance of his exorcisms: "if it is by the Spirit of God that I cast out demons, then the Kingdom of God has come upon you (Matt 12:28).[2] His exorcisms are unlike those effected by "their people" because his casting out of demons is a way by which the reign of God is being effected.  Similarly Jesus employed the symbol of the Kingdom of God to reflect on the condition of the poor: "Blessed are you poor, for yours is the kingdom of God" (Luke 6:20b).[3] The poor are those who have a claim on the support of the just and reigning God.  The evangelical Jesus is also portrayed as reflecting upon the meaning of "traditions".  In the pericope on Real and Traditional Defilement (Matt 15:1-20; par. Mark 7:1-23), Jesus speaks of the selective use of traditions in order to support one's own desires.  He also points to the importance of getting to the heart of the matter.

In his letters, Paul is frequently engaged in theological reflection.  A major case in point would be his lengthy  digression on "spiritual gifts" in

1 Cor 12-14. At the beginning of his reflections, Paul offers the elements of a theological critique.[4] He distinguishes the *charismata* (the "gifts") from the *pneumatica* ("spiritual gifts"). It is the former which are the authentic gifts of the Spirit. Subsequently Paul shows that it is the use to which the charism is put that verifies it as an authentic gift of the Spirit. Yet in 12:3, Paul has already said "that no one speaking by the Spirit of God ever says 'Jesus be cursed' and no one can say 'Jesus is Lord' except by the Holy Spirit."

In terms of the ITT, one can say that the prayer "Jesus is Lord" and the activity of the building up of the church[5] constitute the realities of the syntactic axis which authenticate the charism. In context, the prayer "Jesus is Lord" must be seen as something more than a mere liturgical affirmation. It points to the significance of the human Jesus of Nazareth (in contrast to the neglect of the human Jesus implied in the curse "Jesus be cursed"), faith in the resurrection ("Jesus as Lord"), and a Christian life style (the acceptance of Jesus' Lordship over one's life).[6] The ecclesial use of one's charism is likewise a significant element of the context which points to the authenticity of the charism.

In 1 Cor 12-14, Paul reflects on the "spiritual gifts" both in terms of the church and in terms of his own ministry. In 1 Thes 2, Paul reflects extensively on his own ministry. To do so he utilizes the Scripture (the allusion to Jer 11:20 in v. 4), the example of itinerant preachers (vv. 5,7),[7] the model of the qualified political functionary (v. 4),[8] and the example of the Jewish teachers (v. 11).[9] Elsewhere[10] Paul uses the Scriptures to reflect further on the meaning of his own ministry. For example in the letter to the Roman Paul reflects on the meaning of the mission of proclaiming the Gospel in previously non-evangelized communities by means of Isa 52:15.[11]

This Scriptural precedent, with the examples of Jesus and Paul, serves as a warrant for theological reflection within the contemporary Christian church. However, the importance of theological reflection derives from the very nature of theology itself. In Chapter Three we reflected on experience as a source for theology.[12] Now we might offer some further reflections on the nature of theology. It was Anselm (1033-1109) who described theology as *fides quaerens intellectum* (faith seeking understanding).[13] But what does one understand by *"fides"* (faith)? In the classic treatises on faith, *fides quae* is usually distinguished from *fides qua.* The *fides quae* (faith which) is the content of faith. It is the object of faith. It is the content to which the symbols of the church attest. *Fides qua* (faith by which) is the relationship of faith. It is the relationship which links the believer to the Lord. In classic theological terms, it is subjective faith, that which allows the believer to have objective faith.

While the distinction between *fides quae* and *fides qua* may be useful and while it may enjoy a certain popularity in many theological expositions, it is also quite inadequate. From the *fides quae* and the *fides qua* there should be distinguished a *fides per quam* (faith through which). This is the faith through which we express our belief. It is the existential embodiment of our belief. In his letter to the Galatians, Paul spoke of "faith working through love" πίστις δι' ἀγάπης ἐνεργουμένη, Gal 5:6).[14] The *fides per quam* consists of the many and varied expressions of one's faith in worship and life.

Since marriage is among the primary human relationships, some analogy can be found in the marital relationship which might help to elucidate these three aspects of faith. Primary to marriage is the marriage relationship itself, the union of persons in mutual commitment and support. This aspect of marriage corresponds to the *fides qua.* Upon reflection marriage may be seen to be permanent, exclusive, and procreative. It can be described as a social reality. Such a description of the nature of marriage corresponds to the *fides quae.* But then there are the multiple ways in which the marriage relationship is expressed — sexual interaction, time together, the provision of income, the cooking of meals, shared dreams, and so forth. These are expressive of the marital relationship and can be compared to the *fides per quam.*

That the reality of faith must be looked at in its complexity was underscored a decade ago by Carl Peter who offered some reflections on the question, "What is it to believe as a Christian today?" This American theologian noted that believers have experienced some difficulty in answering this question to their personal satisfaction and further suggested that a threefold inquiry among Roman Catholic theologians corresponds to the believer's personal quest for the understanding of his or her faith. Peter wrote:

"The reality, then, that has given rise to this three-fold inquiry is Christian Faith — in its exercise, content, and norm. As a result, the questions deal with that same faith in a way that corresponds respectively to each of these aspects. Formulated as concisely as possible, they are: (a) In believing as a Christian, what does one do and what precisely happens to one? (Faith as Experience); (b) In the act and experience of Christian believing, just what does one believe? (Faith as Truth Believed); and finally; (c) On what grounds can believing and experiencing this truth be predicated as Christian? (Faith as Verification)."[15]

When "faith as truth believed" is obviously the *fides quae* of traditional theological formulation, "faith as experience" includes both the dimension of *fides per quam* (what one does) and the dimension of *fides qua* (what happens).

In terms of the ITT which we have adopted as a working model for theological reflection, both the symbols which express the *fides quae* and the activities which constitute the *fides per quam* are "signs" which point to a referent, immediately construed as the faith relationship itself (the *fides qua*). On still another level the referent may be taken to be God himself.

In sum, if one is to take as a working definition of theology that theology is "faith seeking understanding", and if the faith which needs elucidation is not only the relationship between humans and God, but also that which is believed about God, and the actions through which the faith relationship is expressed, then theological reflection would seem to be an integral part of the theological endeavor. Indeed, it has always been so, as the examples of Jesus and Paul have indicated.


*Pastorally Necessary*

In the exercise of ministry, the minister must be aware of the specific situation of the church at the present time. For example, *The Tablet* of June 28, 1980[16] offered:

## BASIC FACTS FOR RESPONSIBLE DISCUSSION

| | 1958 | 1968 | 1978 |
|---|---|---|---|
| (1) England & Wales population | 44,977,000 | 47,141,150 | 49,184,000 |
| (2) Estimated Catholic population | 3,277,000 | 4,089,984 | 4,220,750 |
| (3) Total country Mass attendance | Unknown | 1,987,880 | 1,694,175 |
| 3 as percentage of 2 | Unknown | 49% | 32% |
| Priests — | | | |
| Diocesan | | 4,808 ⎫ 7,380 | 4,422 ⎫ 6.797 |
| Religious Orders | 6,789 | 2,572 ⎰ | 2,375 ⎰ |
| Members of religious orders — | | | |
| Women | 15,322 | 13,339 | 12,001 |
| Men | 2,965 | 3,287 | 707 |
| Seminarians | 888 | 865 | 529 |

A similar tableau could be offered for other churches. For example, the diocese of Providence, R.I. (USA) had 116 seminarians enrolled in a four year college seminary program in 1965-1966, but only 21 (of whom 11 were enrolled in the local junior college) enrolled in the analogous program in 1979-1980. In 1981-1982, only seventeen seminarians were participating in the Providence diocesan seminary program at the college level. The diocese of Antwerp (Belgium) which has more than 1,000 ordained priests among its clergy presently has fewer than 10 candidates for the priesthood formation and has no ordained priest less than 30 years of age. In 1983 more than 80% of the priests of the diocese were older than the diocese's fifty year old bishop.

In short, the facts are clear. There are presently fewer ordained ministers in the Roman Catholic Church (churches) that there were a generation ago.[17] The numbers of ordained clergy will continue to decline in the years immediately ahead. But what do these facts mean? For some they are an indication of a lack of faith within the Christian community, or a sign of a lack of generosity on the part of young Christians. For others, these facts are an indication that the Spirit is crying out to the church, pleading with it to accept a wider notion of ministry. Those who adopt this last view interpret the lack of "vocations", not as a lack of vocations as such, but as an indication of vocation to a variety of ministries (the "lay" ministries) and/or as an indication of vocations to a non-celibate priestly ministry. The judgement that one brings to bear on the "facts" is a function of one's ecclesiology. If one's ecclesiology is basically that of the institutional model, with its strong emphasis on the hierarchical ministry, then the present situation is seen as a crisis, because of the lack of priests. If one's basic ecclesiology is framed in terms of a more popularist model, with its emphasis on the ministry of each baptized Christian, then the present situation is seen as an opportunity in which the call of the spirit is embodied.

Thus the "vocation crisis" should not be interpreted only in terms of the church's inability to provide an adequate *cura pastoralis*. A different ecclesiology leads to a different understanding of the present situation. In similar fashion it can be said that different theologies and different anthropologies also lead to different evaluations of the present situation of the church(es).

From this brief description, it is clear that a component of theological reflection is that provided by the social sciences which provide the types of facts with which these remarks began.[18] The very first contribution of the social sciences to the process of theological reflection is the provision of accurate information about a situation or issue that faces the church.[19] Two recent studies devoted respectively to the permanent diaconate[20] and interfaith marriages,[21] published by the National Conference of the Catholic Bishops (USA) can be cited as examples of the provision of empirical data, necessary for pastoral decisions and pastoral planning.

That the data provided by the social sciences must be taken into account for effective pastoral planning is an indication that the church must be engaged in theological reflection if it is to be pastorally effective and true to itself (that is, faithful to its mission). Through ministry the minister expresses the church as a sign of the Kingdom of God:

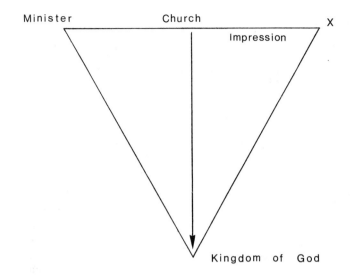

Minister        Church        X

Impression

Kingdom of God

Ultimately theological reflection is done in order that the minister be pastorally effective and that the church be church.

Ultimately, pastoral reflection involves the authenticity of the church. It was Cyprian of Carthage (ca. 258) who said that "custom without truth is the senility of error" (*consuetudo sine veritate est vestustas erroris*).[22] If the church is to exist "in spirit and in truth,"[23] it must subject its practice to reflection in order to ascertain whether it signifies the truth or is in danger of signifying the senility of error. Perhaps one can draw some insight into the importance of theological reflection by pondering the provocative title of Michael Winter's little book, *Mission or Maintenance*.[24] Is the church called to maintain the status quo? Or is the church inherently called to mission? The question is important. If the answer is to be found in the second alternative, theological reflection is of the essence of the church.

Theological reflection is an exercise in pastoral responsibility which is, in fact, necessary for the church. Theological reflection is necessary because we cannot maintain the past. Ministry is a present action which cannot ape the past. We simply cannot stem the tide of history, the real context within which ministry is done. Indeed each and every time that we act (ministerially) we have changed the context within which

91

ministry is done.

Moreover, we ought not to try to maintain the past. Such an attempt is irrational because it is doomed to futility. It is inconsistent with the history of the church which has ever accomodated itself to new social, cultural, and historical circumstances. Indeed, the attempt to maintain the past in the face of the inbreaking of the future denies that the future has, in some measure, been entrusted to our care. It implies a deficient anthropology, one in which human responsibility for the future is neglected.

To cite but one example of the inappropriateness of the attempt to maintain the past in the light of changing circumstances, I can mention an incident that occurred during a graduate course in sacramentology which I offered during the late sixties, a time when serious discussion was taking place as to the appropriate theological language for reflection on the Eucharist. Should we speak of transsubstantiation, transsignification, or transfinalization?[25] One of the students was a young woman who was eventually to pursue a career in nuclear physics. To her, the language of transsubstantiation made no sense at all. She said, "substance is what you analyze scientifically. The 'substance' of the bread does not change during the celebration of the Eucharist." Thus she found the language of transsubstantiation not only inappropriate but also nonsensical.

In short, theological reflection is necessary in order that we "plan the fulfillment of the church for the present and the future."[26] Theological reflection is necessary for the growth of the church. If the church is to move and develop, if it is to change and grow, it must be involved in theological reflection. This growth must be seen as a growth in depth as well as in breadth. The growth of the church should be seen not only in terms of missionary efforts undertaken in order to bring Christianity to those who are as yet unbaptized, it must also be seen as an effort to bring a greater degree of understanding and a greater intensity of commitment to those who are already baptized. Growth in each of these directions (the horizontal as well as the vertical) effectively requires adequate theological reflection.

All this implies that theological reflection has not only a diagnostic function; it has also a critical function. This critical function is to be exercised in view of the church's authenticity and growth. We must come to know not only what is; we must also evaluate what is in terms of what ought to be. In terms of Lonergan's levels of cognition, theological reflection is concerned not only with understanding, it is also concerned with judgment. It is a process that must be conducted on both the intellectual and rational levels in order that decisions can be made on the level of responsibility.[27]

### Personally Useful

For one engaged in ministry within the church, theological reflection does not only serve an ecclesial function, it is also personally useful. In this regard, Laurence O'Connell has written that "theological reflection is the vehicle of growth in ministry, both in terms of personal identity and practical effectiveness."[28] That theological reflection improves one's ministerial effectiveness is apparent insofar as appropriate theological reflection serves to facilitate the church's growth. Thus theological reflection should serve to provide the church's minister with a certain sense of job satisfaction, with a sense of accomplishment. To the extent that theological reflection serves an effective ministry, it contributes to the minister's experience of having faithfully performed the task entrusted to him or to her.[29] Theological reflection's contribution to "job satisfaction" is, in a sense, twofold. On the one hand, theological reflection undertaken prior to the doing of ministry will enable that ministry to be more effective. On the other hand, theological reflection undertaken subsequent to a ministerial experience will enable the minister to evaluate accurately the true effectiveness of that ministry. Beyond this general satisfaction with one's ministerial effectiveness, theological reflection will prove to be personally useful in at least two other regards.

First of all, theological reflection allows one to discern one's own operative theology. One's world view and one's experience interact. There is a relationship between one's being and one's doing. *Agere sequitur esse*, said the scholastic philosophers. One's activity corresponds to one's being. Accordingly, it can be said that one's activity reveals one's own thinking (values, priorities, and so forth), one's vision, eventually one's vision of oneself. "You will know them by their fruits."[30]

Positively, theological reflection allows one's faith perception, that is, one's operative theology, to influence more fully one's personal and social life. To the extent that one reflects critically on one's theology in the context of a faith commitment, one's theological vision will permeate more thoroughly one's life and its activities. Negatively, it must be admitted that "ministry that lacks a clear, expressed theoretical base usually falls victim to one or more traps that renders it ineffective."[31] Urban T. Holmes, late dean of the School of Theology at Sewanee, identified three of the traps[32] in these terms: (1) to function unproductively as a transference object for the neurotic conflict within others (authoritarian figure, scapegoat, guilt provoker, whipping boy, and so forth); (2) to become a "firefighter" (the ministry of reaction, in which the minister responds to each stimulus); and, (3) to buy out of confusion at any price (including the abandonment of the Gospel, which sometimes occurs in those who uncritically accept their model of ministry from the so-called helping professions).

"Burnout"[33] is a phenomenon frequently found in the church's ministers today. Too often they attempt to be "all things to all men,"[34] with the result that there is no time for family, friends, self, renewal. At bottom one might suggest that the root cause of such hyperactivity is a lack of faith. Oftentimes the minister acts as if personal justification comes from the amount of activity that is done on behalf of the Lord. Frequently a minister will act as if he or she has to do everything by him or herself, forgetting that the Lord does everything in his good time and that the minister is but his instrument. Such hyperactivity usually results from a failure to discern the specificity of one's charism.[35] The Whiteheads have suggested a "Christian asceticism of time" as a valuable component of theological reflection,[36] one that can help to avoid ministerial burnout.

A lack of "job satisfaction" within ministry can easily lead to a lack of personal satisfaction, a lack of the sense of one's personal worth. This is personally debilitating. It easily provokes an identity crisis within the minister. Indeed it easily leads to dissatisfaction with the ministry itself, sometimes even to dissatisfaction with the Christian life.

Secondly, theological reflection can contribute to a healthy sense of pastoral and personal identity. A theological student who is engaged in theological reflection might discover, for example, that his or her motives for committing oneself to ministry are theologically or practically untenable. This may lead to the decision to abandon the pursuit of ministry as a specific way of life. This possibility points to the importance of theological reflection in a program of priestly formation or the program of formation for the religious life. One's pastoral program should consist of much more than the mechanics of "doing ministry". It also should lead to a reflection upon what this ministry means to the church, what this ministry means to the future minister.

For one already involved in ministry, theological reflection is, according to Laurence O'Connell, the "crucible in which she (and he) periodically tests the validity of her claim to be a genuine minister of the Lord."[37] In theological reflection one critically evaluates the personal integrity and propriety of one's ministerial activity vis-a-vis theology, Sacred Scripture, and contemporary culture. This critique may (and usually will) lead to some modification. For example, a change in one's life style and/or fashion of doing ministry, due to a refocusing of one's priorities, or a change in the locale of one's ministry, or, finally, the abandonment of one's ministry (in the narrow sense of a specific full-time ministry). In effect theological reflection serves as a form of ministerial examination of conscience. It is a check-up of one's ministerial health, somewhat analogous to a medical examination.

This self-critical testing of the validity of one's claim to be an authentic minister of the Lord is an aspect of the prophetic function of theological reflection, but there is another aspect of theological reflection which enters in when one is reflecting theologically on one's self and which ought not to be neglected. This is the constitutive function of theological reflection.[38] It leads to a confirmation of one's sense of worth and (ministerial) identity. One arrives at the awareness that one really is a more or less authentic minister of the Lord. One perceives what is happening to one's self by reason of the Father's action in and through one's ministry, a ministry which is effective because the power of the Spirit is operative in it. As theological reflection is done in this constitutive manner, one comes to understand that one is who one is because he or she has been called by the Lord, indeed called by name.[39]

Nonetheless, all thinking human beings, including ministers of the Gospel, are victims of self-delusion to some degree. We have learned to rationalize so well. This is particularly inappropriate for the minister whose ministry is perceived by others with the church as an expression of divine concern. "Subjectivism", Holmes wrote, "involves us in a *solipsism* [my emphasis], where one act of ministry becomes as good as another because there are no criteria beyond our personal feelings."[40] As an element of personal ministerial self-evaluation, theological reflection should be both personal and mutual. Moreover, it must include both a positive evaluation and a negative critique. All four elements must be included in an adequate theological reflection since theological reflection is always effected in view of growth, the growth of the church, and the personal and ministerial growth of the church's minister.

1.  See above, p. 58, n. 13.

2.  Par. Luke 11:20; cf. Matt 12:22-32; Luke 11:14-23.

3.  Par. Matt 5:3. Cf. Jacques Dupont, *Les Béatitudes*, 2.
    *La Bonne Nouvelle. Etudes bibliques* (Paris: Gabalda,
    1969) pp. 92-122; Herman Hendrickx, *Sermon on the
    Mount* (Manila: East Asian Pastoral Institute, 1979),
    pp. 15-18.

4.  See Ernst Käsemann, *Essays on New Testament Themes.
    Studies in Biblical Theology*, 41 (London: SCM,
    1964), p. 66.

5.  Eph 4:12.

6.  Eph 5:21-6:9; comp. Col 3:18-4:1.

7.  See A. J. Malherbe, "'Gentle as a Nurse'. The Cynic
    Background to I Thes ii," *Novum Testamentum* 12
    (1970) 203-217.

8.  See A.-M. Denis, "L'Apôtre Paul, prophète
    'messianique' des Gentiles, Etude thématique de
    I Thes II, 1-6," *Ephemerides Theologicae Lovanienses*
    33 (1957) 245-318, pp. 209-303.

9.  See R. F. Collins, "Paul, as seen through his own
    eyes. A Reflection on the First Letter to the
    Thessalonians," *Louvain Studies* 8 (1980-1981)
    348-381, pp. 356-364.

10. For example in Rom 10:14-15, v. 15.

11. See Rom 15:17-21, v. 21.

12. See above, pp. 35-40.

13. Augustine had said "*Desideravi intellectu videre
    quod credidi*" (I desired to see with my
    understanding that which I believed) (*De Trinitate*,
    XV, 28, 51; PL 42, 1098; English Translation in
    *The Fathers of the Church*, 45 (Washington: Catholic
    University of America, 1962) p. 523). Nonetheless
    the *fides quaerens intellectum* formulation is
    generally associated with Anselm, one of the
    earliest of the schoolmen. Anselm originally gave
    to his work, the *Proslogion*, the title *Fides
    Quaerens Intellectum*. In the early part of this
    work he wrote: "*Non tento, Domine, penetrare
    altitudinem tuam; quia nullatenus comparo illi*

*intellectum meum, sed desidero aliquatenus
intelligere veritatem tuam, quam credit et amat cor
meum. Neque enim quaero intelligere, ut credam;
sed credo, ut intelligam...* " ("I will not attempt
to penetrate your greatness because my intellect is
in no way comparable to it, but I would like to
understand something of your truth, which my heart
believes and loves. For I do not seek to
understand in order to believe; rather I believe in
order that I might understand... ") (*Proslogion*
I, 2; PL 158, 227).

14. See also Jas 2:14-17.

15. C. Peter, *art. cit.*, p. 87.

16. *The Tablet* 234 (1980) 638.

17. See Nicholas Walsh, "The Challenge of the Vatican
    Statistics," *Origins* 12 (1982) 425-427.

18. The point has been made by André G. Van
    Campenhoudt in an address on "The Local Churches".
    Van Campenhoudt stated: "When a pastoral decision
    has to be made, the appeal to theology is not
    enough, for today, more than ever, all decision
    making requires a precise, scientific knowledge of
    reality, and it is not the role of theology, but
    rather than of the social sciences to provide us
    with such information" (Brussels: Prospective,
    1975).

19. The Whiteheads have identified three additional
    contributions of the social sciences to the process
    of theological reflection, as follows: (2) the
    religious tradition can define a problem according
    to its own criteria and then use social science
    research methods to test a hypothesis or to achieve
    a more accurate description of the problem. [See,
    for example, Eugene C. Kennedy - Victor J. Heckler,
    *The Loyola Psychological Study of the Ministry and
    Life of the American Priest* (Washington: NCCB,
    1971)]; (3) the religious tradition can adopt the
    techniques and tools developed in the social
    sciences for use in pursuit of its own goals; and,
    (4) the social sciences can provide information and
    interpretation on questions that are of independent
    interest to the religious community. See J. D.
    Whitehead - E. E. Whitehead, *op. cit.*, pp. 75-76.

20. *A National Study of the Permanent Diaconate in the United States* (Washington: NCCB, 1981).

21. Dean R. Hoge - Kathleen M. Ferry, *Empirical Research on Interfaith Marriage in America* (Washington: NCCB, 1981).

22. (*Ep. 74*, par. 9). See further *Ep.* 71, pars. 2-3; *Ep.* 73, par. 13. Of these only *Ep.* 71 is printed in Magne, *Patrologia Latina*, 4 (p. 410). English translations of the pertinent passages can be found in *The Fathers of the Church*, 51. *Saint Cyprian. Letters (1-81)* (Washington: Catholic University of America, 1964), pp. 264, 275-276, 292.

23. John 4:23; see further Eucharistic Prayer I, "an offering in spirit and in truth."

24. Michael M. Winter, *Mission or Maintenance. A Study in New Pastoral Structures* (London: Darton, Longman & Todd, 1973).

25. See Joseph M. Powers, *Eucharistic Theology* (New York: Herder and Herder, 1967); Paul VI, Encyclical Letter *Mysterium Fidei* (September 3, 1965), in *The Papal Encyclicals 1958-1981*, 165-177, esp. par. 11, p. 166.

26. H. Schuster, *art. cit.*, pp. 12-13.

27. See above, pp. 16, 52-53.

28. L. J. O'Connell, *art. cit.*, p. 169.

29. See 2 Tim 4:7-8.

30. Matt 7:16, 20; 12:23; cf. Luke 6:43-45.

31. Urban T. Holmes, "An Outline of an Intentional Theory of Ministry," *The St. Luke's Journal of Theology* 20 (1977) 85-97, p. 85.

32. *Idem.*, pp. 85-86.

33. See Norbert Brockman, "Burnout in Superiors," *Review for Religious* 37 (1978) 809-816. Cf. "The Priest and Stress," a report issued by the U.S. Bishops' Committee on Priestly Life and Ministry in *Origins* 11 (1982) 661-667.

34. 1 Cor 9:29.

35. Cf. 1 Cor 12:7-11.

36. See J. D. Whitehead, "A Christian Asceticism of Time," Chapter 10 in *Method in Ministry*, pp. 145-164; James D. Whitehead, "An Asceticism of Time," *Review for Religious* 39 (1980) 3-17.

37. L. J. O'Connell, *art. cit.*, p. 167.

38. The prophetic and constitutive functions of theological reflection in regards to this ministry and person are somewhat analogous to the prophetic and constitutive functions of the scriptural word in the development of the total constitution of the Scriptures as a constitutive element of the church. On this point, see James A. Sanders, "Hermeneutic," in *Interpreter's Dictionary of the Bible*, suppl., ed. by Keith Crim (Nashville: Abingdon, 1976) 402-407, pp. 404-405.

39. See Jer 1.

40. U. T. Holmes, *art. cit.*, p. 88.

Chapter Seven


A Brief Summary


At the conclusion of these six chapters on the theoretical underpinnings of a method of theological reflection, some summary remarks might prove helpful in the quest to identify and articulate the nature and purpose of theological reflection. Drawing inspiration from the early contributions of the Whiteheads as well as from the *Program of Priestly Formation*, Louis Brusatti offered "significant insights" [his expression] on theological reflection as follows. (1) The Underlying method is derived from an Action/Reflection model with a resulting 'new' integrational synthesis. (2) Theological Reflection is an on-going and dialogic, individual and group process. (3) Participants or actors in the process include the individual/group reflector(s); existential experience, both individual and communal; and Scripture and the on-going tradition of the Church. (4) Theological Reflection has a future orientation about it — a calling the kingdom forth. (5) From an individual perspective theological reflection is an integrating factor calling one to personalize his/her theology and God-relationship. (6) ... a two directional method: 'The student learns how to allow his experience to question his theological tradition as well as how to allow the tradition to confront his experience.'"[1]

These statements identify six of the principal characteristics of theological reflection. Theological reflection is nothing more than "faith experience seeking understanding". It is a matter of "making sense of ministry". Its method is essentially dialogical. Positively, it includes a diagnostic component; negatively, it implies a critical function. On the scale of the levels of cognition, theological reflection is to be located on the levels of understanding and judgement. The first level of cognition, experience, constitutes the object of theological reflection, while the fourth level, responsibility, points to the purpose of theological reflection. That purpose, briefly stated, but in the broadest of perspectives, is that the church might be Church. Alternatively, expressed, the purpose of theological reflection is that a ministerial experience might be *theologia*. To be effective, theological reflection must be exercised both individually and mutually. When theological reflection is effected in this fashion it results in a greater self-awareness of the minister and the growth of the church.

As a model of theological reflection, we have adopted the ITT. It is a model which looks to the church as a sign, and asks not only what is the meaning of this sign but how does this sign convey its meaning, how is it meaningful.

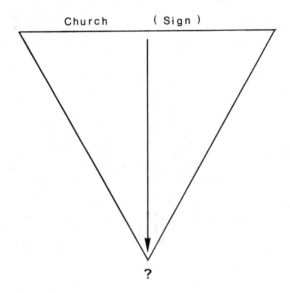

Church        ( Sign )

?

Within the church, the various activities of its ministers are so many signs which constitute the global sign which is the church itself. Each of these ministerial activities can therefore be profitably analyzed by means of the ITT. One can ask, what is the (specific) meaning of this (concrete) sign; how does it convey its meaning.

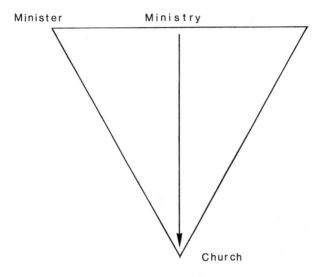

Minister          Ministry

Church

Although the model of the ITT is borrowed from the field of semiotics,[2] it would seem especially useful as a model for theological reflection. On the one hand, it is both scientific and contemporary. On the other hand, it is an apt tool for analyzing the function of a sign, and the church, from a theological standpoint, is to be considered as a "sign".[3] In the language of the Magisterium, the church is a "sort of sacrament".[4] If a sign is a "sacrament" in the traditional theological jargon, we can note that a sign is a "metaphor" in the jargon of the linguists. A metaphor has a fashion of communicating a message that is quite specific and rather appropriate to itself.

The search for metaphorical truth[5] is different from the search for scientific truth. It is different from the search for philosophical truth. It is even different from the search for that truth which is the object of systematic theology. In view of this, it can be said that theological reflection is undertaken as a search for the metaphor which is apt to express that which we really believe.

1. Louis T. Brusatti, C. M., "Theological Reflection and Erikson's Developmental Framework," in *Theological Field Education*, 151-164, p. 151.

2. This adoption of the ITT model represents, in fact, a modality of the third type of contribution of the social sciences to the process of theological reflection. See above, p. 97, n. 19.

3. See above, p. 33.

4. *Lumen Gentium*, 1.

5. See above, p. 69.

# Part    Two


# Five    Models

Chapter Eight


The Efficiency Model


*A Reflection on Church Renewal*
*after Vatican II*

After the presentation of the theoretical base of
the present approach to theological reflection, we can
consider several different models for theological
reflection. Each of these models reflects an *"angle of*
*vision"*. Thus we are dealing more with a "type of
model" than with a single model. As an overarching
model and useful paradigm, the ITT will always be on the
horizon. One of its salient features is the reminder
that semiosis, the conveying of meaning, is a single
process. Accordingly, the five models which will be
analyzed in the second part of this work are actually
five interlocking models. One must not be separated
from the other, even if, for purpose of analysis, one
angle of vision must temporarily be considered in
relative isolation from the others. As we proceed to
the first model, the efficiency model, it rapidly
appears that its angle of vision is the pragmatic axis
(specifically the element of expression) of the ITT.


*Some Examples*

As part of the renewal of the church following the
Second Vatican Council, many attempts were made to
update the life of the church and formation of its
ministers. A variety of techniques was borrowed from
the various social sciences in order to provide for a
more efficient ministry within the church.


*Example One: Seminary classes*
*in communication*

Since the *Decree on Priestly Formation* urged that
seminarians "be carefully instructed in those matters
which have a special bearing on the sacred ministry,
especially catechetics, preaching... "[1] most seminaries
instituted courses in homiletics or radically modified

the traditional training in "Sacred Eloquence".

Frequently these new courses included the use of video-tapes to provide for a "replay" of a homily which could be "objectively" experienced by the homilist himself and thus subject to dialogue and critical analysis. Often selected members of the laity were invited to view the "replay" as a prelude to offering their critique. This type of dialogue and analysis was often called "theological reflection". The reflection commonly focused on the technique of the homily, its method. Attention was paid to gestures and eye contact, the use of metaphors and examples. Both the method of reflection ("replay" and "feedback") and the content of the reflection suggest that the angle of vision for reflection on the homily was "efficiency". Was it clear and captivating? The criteria for judging the successful homily were those of the secular world of communications.

The method of teaching homiletics (catechetics, religious education, and other related efforts) was also a borrowed one. The course content was often taken from the world of communications workshops. In these workshops, the focus was generally on the "process" rather than the object of the process. In the homiletics class, the focus of attention was often "the form" rather than "the content". I personally experienced a striking result of this approach to homiletics training in a homily delivered during the course of the Sunday eucharistic liturgy to a large congregation back in 1969. The homily had been prepared for the occasion during the intern deacon's last semester in seminary. The homily was a gem of clear language. The gestures, the pauses, the metaphors, the examples were perfect. Its topic was the church — yet not once did the homilist mention "God", "Jesus", or "faith".

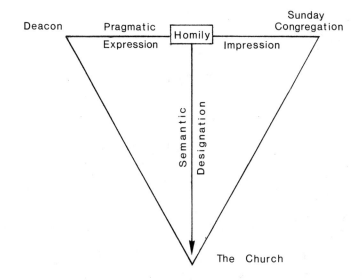

Along the pragmatic axis of expression, the homily
was nearly perfect. The homilist's expression was
"excellent". Along the semantic axis, there was
relatively little meaning conveyed. At most one would
draw the conclusion that the church was another
fraternal organization, similar to the Elks or the
Moose.

*Example Two:  Parish organizations*

In the mid-seventies, one American diocese of my
acquaintance committed itself fully to diocesan-wide
renewal on the parish and deanery level.[2]  An Office of
Planning and Development was established. A "Think
Tank" was set up. An outside resource person was
brought in, in order to assist each of the parishes of
the diocese to assume responsibility for its future by
means of pastoral planning. The method urged was that
of goal-setting. Long term goals were to be identified
within each parish. These were to be reached by means
of concrete objectives, to be realized within a shorter
time frame. A system of accountability (checks and
evaluation) was built into the program, which was
celebrated in a paraliturgical service. During a prayer
service held in the diocesan cathedral, "parish
charters" were presented by the bishop to the pastors
of the various parishes.[3]  Appropriate charts
(organizational charts, management charts, etc.) were

provided to assist parishes in the task at hand. By way of example, some of these charts are offered on the following pages.[4]

## REFINED PRESENT MODEL
### ORGANIZATION CHART

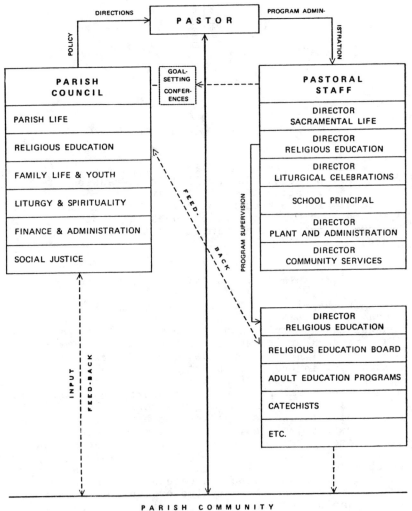

# REFINED PRESENT MODEL
## MODEL MANAGEMENT PLAN FOR A CALENDAR YEAR

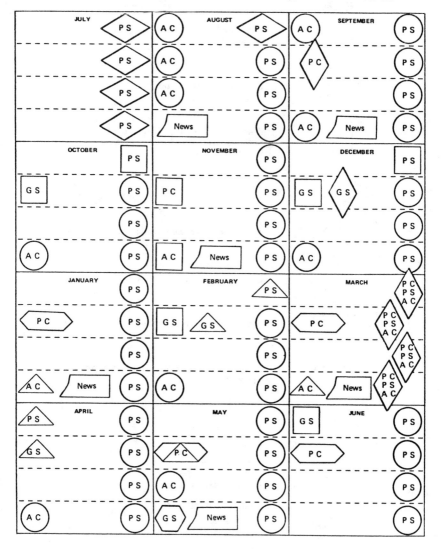

# REFINED PRESENT MODEL
## MANAGEMENT CHART

### SYMBOLS AND ABBREVIATIONS
### FOR CALENDAR CHART

| SYMBOLS | ACTIVITY REPRESENTED |
|---|---|
| ○ | PROGRAM SUPPORT, TRAINING, RECRUITING, COORDINATION |
| △ | GOAL-SETTING OR BUDGETING |
| ▢ | PERFORMANCE EVALUATION AND EFFECTIVE-NESS, IMPACT APPRAISAL, SURVEYS |
| ◇ | PLAN STRATEGIES |
| ◆ | DATA GATHERING AND FEED-BACK |
| ⬡ | DEANERY-LEVEL REVIEW OF GOALS |
| ▱ | PUBLICATION OF INFORMATION (NEWSLETTER) |
| ⬢ | POLICY- AND DECISION-MAKING, PRIORITIES, ALLOCATION |

ABBREVIATIONS

P.S.    PASTORAL STAFF

P.C.    PARISH COUNCIL

A.C.    ACTION COMMITTEE

G.S.    GOAL-SETTING COMMITTEE

# INTERLOCKING TEAMS MODEL
## ORGANIZATION CHART

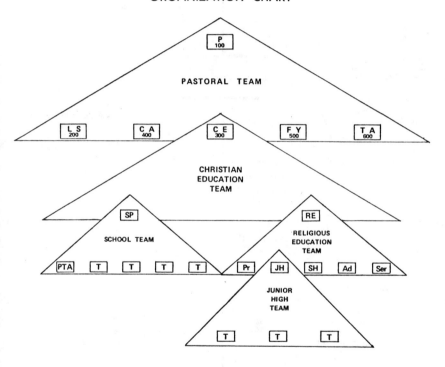

# PASTORAL SERVICE DEANERY SYSTEM

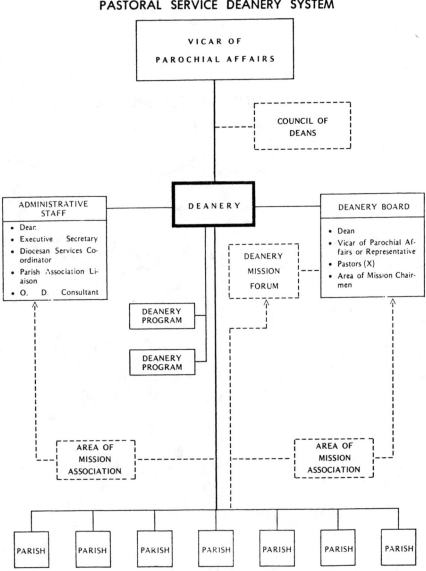

This extensive attempt at parish and diocesan renewal in the diocese which I have cited was similar to the attempts at renewal which took place in other dioceses of the United States.[5] What they shared in common was the appropriation of methods for the improvement of efficiency taken from the business world. Methods of corporation efficiency were borrowed in order to improve the institution of the church. Now, barely a decade later, it appears that these efforts have not achieved the desired results. An analysis of this type of renewal by means of the ITT helps to clarify what really happened.

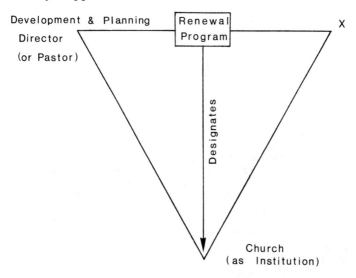

The referent of the renewal effort was clearly the church. The efforts made were in view of the "improvement" of the church ("renewal" was the in-word at the time). Along the syntactic axis, a renewed church structure clearly indicated the church as an institution. The problem was that the method of renewal was one that "implied" big business and corporate structures. Organization, management, and efficiency charts are commonly associated with General Motors and other large corporations. It was corporations such as these that are "implied" by the syntactic axis.

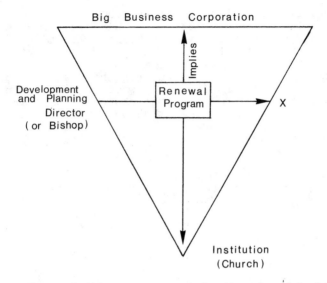

Big Business Corporation

Development and Planning Director (or Bishop)

Renewal Program

Implies

X

Institution (Church)

Thus at the very moment in the church's history when a foundational document such as *Lumen Gentium* was calling for a self-awareness of the "holy mystery of the Church", [6] when people around the world were calling for greater authenticity and personal self-determination, when personalism [7] was the philosophy of the day, the church was projecting an image of itself as a corporate institution along the lines of the multinationals. Is it any wonder that the renewal failed, particularly among a generation of young adults who were rejecting institutional structures as they pursued personal freedom and authenticity? From the point of view of the receiver of the "message" (the impression along the pragmatic axis), the message was that the church was a very efficient temporal structure. Structure and institution, with their power and their anonymity, were, however, the antithesis of the community that many were then seeking as they gropingly retreated from society to the "shelter" of the commune, and its simple life.

*Example Three: Priestly ministry*

During those times of renewal, with its appropriation of borrowed models, Arthur X. Deegan wrote [8] that: "... In one research endeavor, five specific criteria for measuring effectiveness were determined as a result of breaking down the job of the priest, especially the pastor, into five rather

116

arbitrary component parts as follows:

"(1) *Area of financial administration:* is the pastor able to raise and handle funds in such a way that the parish can build the necessary buildings and pay off the debt according to the potential in his area? Does the pastor maintain the standard accounts and accounting reports for the diocese as he should? Does the pastor cooperate in diocesan campaigns according to the potential in his area?

"(2) *Human relations area:* is the pastor able to administer to the parish effectively (get results) and yet not forget the human dignity of assistant pastors, employees, and parishioners? Measure the pastor by any interpersonal problems he might have had with the assistant pastors, complaints from the clergy, or laity, or his overall general reputation for handling people as known generally in the diocese.

"(3) *General administrative capacity:* does the pastor have a reputation for completing assignments on schedule, meeting deadlines, getting in reports, carrying out projects, being punctual and thorough?

"(4) *Attitude of cooperation regarding superiors:* does the pastor strive to carry out in his parish all diocesan directives, policies, projects, as a member of a larger team?

"(5) *Self improvement area:* does the pastor seek to improve his own knowledge and skills in administrative-pastoral matters? Does he attend conferences, initiate study programs, seek professional advancement?"

Taking a cue from Douglas McGregor's book, *The Human Side of Enterprise*, Doctor Deegan analyzed two styles of leadership:[9]

| STYLES OF SUPERVISION | | |
|---|---|---|
| STYLE: | A  Autocratic  M | Developmental  D |
| Often called... | BOSS | LEADER |
| Motivates from... | FEAR | INSPIRATION |
| Supervision is... | CLOSE | GENERAL |

117

At the time of writing *The Priest as Manager*,
Deegan was Director of the Office of Planning and
Research for the Archdiocese of Detroit. He offered the
"Management by Objectives" Technique (MBO) as a means to
help the pastor arrive at decisions about raising money,
increasing attendance at CCD meetings, solving the
problem of late-comers at Mass, and finding better
teachers for the parish school. As a typical schedule
for the installation of an MBO system, Deegan[10] offered
the following example.

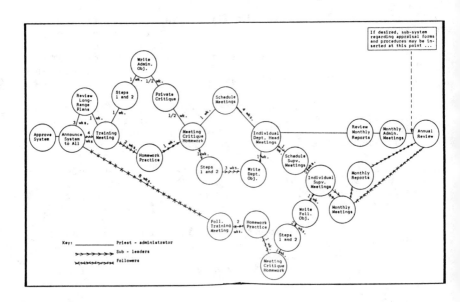

To be sure, Deegan rejected the notion that a priest should be a "carbon copy of a General Motors executive". The method that he offered was simply intended to increase priestly efficiency. Yet once again, were the method offered to be analyzed along the syntactic axis of the ITT, it would appear that the priest was being cast in the model of the business executive. His activities and aims were similar to theirs.

When analyzing these examples of renewal of the parish and the priestly ministry by means of the ITT, it appears that the church projected itself to the onlooker in the guise of a business corporation and that the church leader was projected as a sort of business executive. The criterion for evaluating both the institution and its ministers was the criterion of the efficiency of production. This should lead to the question what type of business is the church in? What is its product? If the church is a "mystery", is its "product" quantifiable?

To raise these types of questions is to offer a theological critique of the renewal of the American church in the decade which followed upon the close of the Second Vatican Council. At this point we can forgo this type of critique, because the primary purpose of the present chapter is simply to elucidate the use of the ITT as a model for analyzing the experience of the American church in the 1965-1975 decade. The burden of the present chapter belongs to the understanding level of cognition rather than the judgmental.

*Example Four:*

*The Rite of Reconciliation*

In accordance with the provisions of Paragraph 72 of the Conciliar Decree, *Sacrosanctum Concilium*, "The rite and formulas for the sacrament of penance are to be revised so that they may give more luminous expression to both the nature and effect of the sacrament,"[11] the rite of reconciliation was reformed as of December 2, 1973. The renewal of the rite may be schematized according to the ITT in this manner:

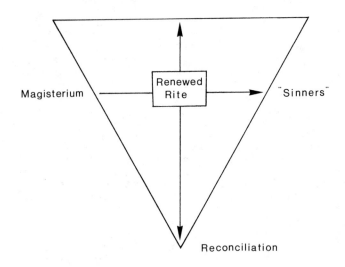

Along the pragmatic axis, the renewal of the ritual of reconciliation was fantastic. A clearer "expression" was given to the sacrament. The sacrament was to be celebrated in the vernacular, in order that the faithful could more readily understand it and more fully participate in it. Instead of "confession" in a dark confessional box, the rite of reconciliation was ideally to be celebrated in a face-to-face encounter and the "confessor" was urged to make a tactile gesture of acceptance of the "sinner". In this fashion reconciliation with the church was effectively dramatized. That the rite was a sacrament, and therefore a form of liturgical prayer, was to be expressed in a prayerful liturgical reading of the Scriptures prior to the confession of sin. The location and decor of the reconciliation room was to add to the liturgical setting of the rite. A variety of modes of celebrating reconciliation were also indicated: individual auricular confession, a penitential prayer service, general absolution. From the standpoint of expression (that is along the pragmatic axis, from the standpoint of the sender of the message), the renewed rite of reconciliation was henceforth to be a marvelous "celebration".

The facts are that since the 1973 renewal of the rite of reconciliation, the sacrament has been celebrated by fewer and fewer persons and at a much lower rate of frequency than existed in the church until the time of renewal. This should not be taken as a call to return to the "old way"[12] of doing things, rather it is a call for theological reflection. Why hasn't the renewal renewed the penitential spirit of the church? Why hasn't it contributed to a greater sense of the need for reconciliation? In sum, why hasn't the renewal "worked"? A look at the ITT schema can provide material for some enlightening reflection.

The referent of the rite renewed is reconciliation. In fact, the reconciliation celebrated in the sacrament of reconciliation is threefold: reconciliation to God, reconciliation to the church, reconciliation to oneself. From the vantage point of sacramental theology, reconciliation with God is achieved in and through reconciliation with the church. That is the burden of the sacrament of reconciliation as a sacrament. Broadly speaking these three dimensions of sacramental reconciliation can be summed up under the rubrics of forgiveness, absolution, and conversion/repentence. One seeks reconciliation in order to find peace with God, peace with the community of the church, and peace with oneself.

These three dimensions of reconciliation correspond to the triple alienation which is called sin in our religious tradition. Sin is an "offense" against God insofar as it is a "violation of his law", the refusal to follow his will, or the misuse of his gifts. Sin is an "offense" against the community, either in the narrower sense of an explicit offense to those who are hurt by one's sin, or in the broader sense of the church whose ministry of witness is compromised by the sin of the members of the church.[13] Finally sin is an offense against oneself insofar as (serious) sin represents a turning from one's "final end" or an alienation from one's authentic self. Thus one can speak of a triple alienation provoked by sin — the alienation from God, the alienation from the church, and the alienation from oneself. The threefold character of the reconciliation corresponds to this triple alienation.

Now one must ask whether the faithful, who still identify "sin"[14] by means of the categories of the catechisms with which they were instructed while still very young, experience this threefold alienation when they sin.

(1) *Alienation from God.* Oftentimes thinking members of the laity have been heard to say, "I think it's alright, but it's a 'sin'." What this statement implies is, on the one hand, a judgment in conscience

that the action under consideration is morally correct,
and, on the other hand, the application of traditional
catechetical categories to the action under
consideration. In fact, an adequate theology of sin
suggests that an action is sinful because it is morally
evil (rather than its being morally wrong because it is
a "sin"). Because the judgment in conscience is
correct, the person who performs such an action hardly
experiences him or herself as sinful and thereby somehow
alienated from God. Oftentimes such a person will
affirm that, before God, he or she acted as best as he
or she could. In such a case, the person does not
experience himself as alienated from God, even though
verbally acknowledging that he or she has "sinned".

(2) *Alienation from the community.* One's
significant group, one's peer group, is all important in
the formation of one's conscience.[15] Within the Roman
Catholic community, the importance of the community as a
significant element in conscience formation was
experienced in the days after the publication of
Paul VI's encyclical letter, *Humanae Vitae.*[16] It was
not only that vast numbers of persons who were not Roman
Catholics considered artificial contraception to be a
morally legitimate means of family planning, but also
that many Roman Catholics themselves considered
contraception to be a legitimate means of fulfilling the
vocation of responsible parenthood. Rather than
experiencing alienation from the community as a result
of their judgment in conscience on contraception, many
Roman Catholics experienced a feeling of identification
with others in the Roman Catholic community.[17]

(3) *Alienation from the self.* Oftentimes those
who are involved in activities that have been classified
as "sinful" consider that they have done what had to be
done in a given situation. They feel as if they have
been acting in accord with what is best in them. They
think that they have been true to themselves. Thus
there is no real experience of alienation from the self,
no true experience of dis-ease as a result of "sin".

In sum, oftentimes in our days the positing of
actions which have traditionally been classified as
"sinful" is not experienced as alienation-producing,
that is as truly sinful. On the other hand, many
instances of egregious social evil have not been
classified as "sin". Indeed, some situations in which
there is a tremendous objective moral evil are justified
in traditional theological categories, by means of the
principle of the double effect. Thus the real evil

which exists in our world was and is oftentimes not expressed in terms of the "sin" category.

In effect, the receiver of the church's teaching on the reform of the rite of reconciliation was often not experiencing the rite as a needed form of reconciliation in the wake of true evil. The "sign" is ambiguous because of confusion along the syntactic axis. Reconciliation is appropriate when sin-provoked alienation exists but true alienation does not exist when some "sin" is present. On the other hand, true alienation exists when a major moral evil is present but then reconciliation is not really appropriate because this is not a matter of "sin"-provoked alienation. Because of this confusion along the semantic axis, the reformed rite of reconciliation does not make an "impression" along the pragmatic axis on those for whom the "sign" (the message of the renewed rite) was intended.

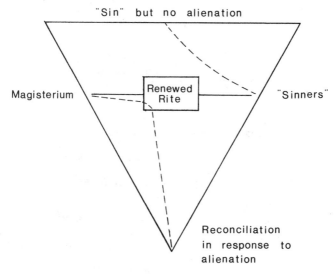

Because "sinners" do not experience "sin" as provoking alienation, they cannot experience the rite of reconciliation as an experience of reconciliation. Hence, the rite of reconciliation has become for many, a relatively insignificant part of their Christian experience.

On the other hand, there are those who have virtually abandoned the practice of the rite of reconciliation because they do not perceive the connection between the rite of reconciliation and moral evil. For many of these individuals the rite of reconciliation is another example of the insignificance (that is, the lack of significance) of the church's ritual, and ultimately of the church itself. Thus:

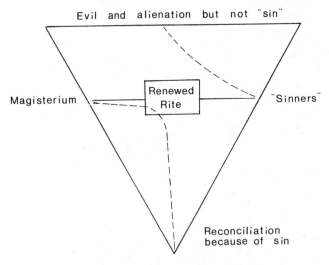

Still, there are many Catholic Christians who continue to participate in the rite of reconciliation. Many of these continue to do so because the sacrament of reconciliation, albeit celebrated in a new form, is a traditional and grace-giving rite of the church. Their perception of the sacrament is simply the perception of a church rite, somewhat independently of its specificity. The meaning of the rite lies in the fact that it is a rite of the church — hardly anything more or less. Their perception of the sacrament is similar to the attitude of those who value the church's rite for ecclesiastical ritual's sake. The attitude of "rite for rite's sake" exists among many church-goers, albeit in varying degrees. It is present in those who seek baptism for their infant children but do not intend to rear them in the faith, as well as in those who want to be married "in church", but do not intend to take part in the life of the church as a sacramentally married couple. To some lesser degree it is present in those who look to the sacrament of orders as an important rite but who do not look beyond it to the ministry which it ought to entail. In the case of those who opt for the celebration of the ritual of reconciliation for the rite's sake, we have the application of the ITT which is given below. In these cases, the rite may indeed be celebrated with some frequency, but it should be obvious that it is not the renewed rite, as intended by the Magisterium, which is significant.

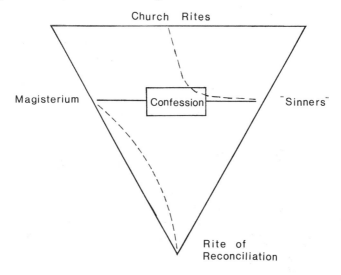

*A Brief Reflection*

The efficiency models of "theological reflection" so often used during the past fifteen years or so, evaluate ministry almost exclusively along the pragmatic axis, with a focus upon the dimension of expression. They are deficient insofar as they neglect the fact that ministry, as significant (that is, meaningful) activity, conveys meaning in a single process. If church renewal is to be effective in a meaningful fashion it must take all foci of the semiotic process into account.

Church renewal which takes place mainly along the pragmatic axis of expression easily provides the recipient of the message with a vision of church as an agent of production or at best, as an institution. This is because of the implications of the sign along the syntactic axis. If, because of these implications, the impression received is of the church as an institution or as an agent of production, further theological reflection is called for. Attention must be paid to the semantic axis. In what sense can the church be seen as an agent of production? Is it grace which is the "product" of the church? If so, what is one's understanding of grace?... If the church is an institution, what is its specificity? From a theological point of view, the institutional elements of the church are necessary to ecclesial existence. Nonetheless a sound theology states that the institutional elements of the church serve the church in its other, more radical capacities.

It should, of course, go without saying that theological reflection and institutional reform along the pragmatic axis is useful, and necessary, to the extent that it is accompanied by theological reflection along the semantic and syntactic axes. The significance of these other dimensions of theological reflection has been equivalently stated by both John Shea and Urban Holmes.

Holmes wrote: "Counselling, group work, community action, and organizational development are not necessarily alien to Christian ministry, but unexamined patterning of ministry after these forms of action may involve the unwitting acceptance of a point of view in direct opposition to the Christian witness."[18] Similarly Shea stated: "Although the helping and change agent abilities are built on assumptions about human nature, systems, and the process of change, there is a way in which they are neutral. They are methods which can be applied to any content. They become components of ministerial theology when they are linked to the theological ability and exercised in relation to the agenda which that ability carries."[19]

While attention to the intended meaning of the sign is present when reflection is exercised along the semantic axis, a full consideration of the meaningfulness of the sign demands that consideration be given to the syntactic axis as well. Reflection must be brought to bear upon those for whom the message is intended in order to grasp the "sign system" which they will associate with a given form of ministry (or renewal of ministry). If one who is engaged in theological reflection, paying due attention to the syntactic axis, comes to the conclusion that the meaning of a sign is one thing for the minister and another thing for the recipients of ministry, then the minister has the responsibility of educating the recipients of ministry, so that they perceive the sign adequately, that is in relation to the sign system which it is intended to imply. Alternatively such reflection may lead to the conclusion that the sign itself must be changed if its "message" is to be heard. Considerations such as these point to the importance of reflection and education in the total process of the effective renewal of ministry.

The thoughts which have been offered thus far, as a brief critique of the efficiency model, point to the fact that a sign produces its meaning as a single total process. In analogous fashion it must be said that church renewal (the reformulation of a sign) is meaningful as a single total process. Church renewal will be effective only if the institutional elements are improved (reform along the pragmatic axis), if the institutional elements more clearly signify the referent to which the church ultimately relates (adequacy along the semantic axis), and if those for whom the message of the church is intended are enabled to perceive the meaningfulness of the church because of the associations which they make along the syntactic axis.

In sum, to the question "Is it (a sign, ministry) expressive?" (a reflection along the pragmatic axis, dimension of expression), we must add the questions "Is it clear?" (a reflection along the semantic axis) and "Is it authentic and consistent?" (a reflection along the syntactic axis). All three of these questions must be asked if ministry is to be "impressive", that is, if it is to have a significant effect.

Today many people ask "What went wrong with Vatican II?" or "Why hasn't church renewal been fully effective?" The answer may well lie in the fact that the church's ministers didn't ask enough questions.

1. *Optatam Totius*, 19 in *Documents*, p. 454. See *Dei Verbum*, 24 in *Documents*, p. 127; *Sacrosanctum Concilium*, 52 in *Documents*, p. 155.

2. Cf. John Dreher, ed., *Parish Renewal. Models for Sharing Christ's Mission in the Parish* (Providence: Diocese of Providence, 1975); John Dreher, Maurice St. Pierre, *United in Hope. Models for Deanery Organization. Diocese of Providence* (Providence, Diocese of Providence, 1974).

3. Comparable charters were likewise presented by the bishop to the heads of various diocesan offices and agencies.

4. *Parish Renewal*, pp. 14, 18-19, 22; *United in Hope*, p. 7.

5. See Thomas T. Tewey, *Recycling the Parish* (Washington: National Council of Catholic Laity, 1972).

6. *Lumen Gentium*, 5 in *Documents*, p. 17.

7. See *Gaudium et Spes*, 26 in *Documents*, p. 225.

8. Arthur X. Deegan, *The Priest as Manager* (New York: Bruce, 1969).

9. *Idem.*, p. 63.

10. *Idem.*, pp. 92-93.

11. *Documents*, p. 161.

12. See above, pp. 91-92.

13. When a member of the church "sins", the church "sins" (insofar as one of its qualified ministers, one of its representatives, has sinned) and is "sinned against" (insofar as its witness has been compromised). See *Unitatis Redintegratio*, 4 in *Documents*, p. 348.

14. The reflection on sin which is offered here is rather narrow in its point of view. A fundamental option approach to sin would put the entire discussion in another light. In the judgment of the present author, however, it would appear that the act-centered approach to sin is still that most commonly held by the faithful, particularly among

the older generations of the faithful.

15. Cf. James M. Gustafson, *The Church as Moral Decision Maker* (Philadelphia: Pilgrim, 1976).

16. July 25, 1968.  See *The Papal Encyclicals 1958-1981*, pp. 223-236.

17. In fact, the experience has often been a mixed one— identification with other Catholics, some alienation from the official church.

18. Urban T. Holmes, *art. cit.*, p. 86.

19. John Shea, "Doing Ministerial Theology," p. 193.

Chapter Nine


The Ecclesial Model


*What Kind of a Church Do You Want?*

In the previous chapter, we examined a variety of
recent experiences within the church which were intended
to lead to a renewal of the church.  To a large extent
these innovations did not achieve the desired result.
On analysis it was found that many of these endeavors
did not sufficiently take into account the fact that
effective signing requires attention to the total
semiotic process, not only to the dimension of
expression along the pragmatic axis.

It was also suggested that concern with the
efficiency of the church, and the subsequent reflection
on that efficiency, easily conveys the message that the
church is a production-oriented organization.  A two-
fold question should now arise.  Is that understanding
of the church the one which the ministers of the church
are inevitably bound to project?  Is that understanding
of church the one which the ministers of the church
ought to project?

Indeed, "what kind of Church do you want?"[1] is a
question that the members of the church might put to the
leaders and ministers of the church.  In attempting some
summary formulation of a response, the thoughts advanced
by Avery Dulles in *Models of the Church*[2] will prove
quite helpful.  In this little volume, Dulles has
provided a comprehensive overview of ecclesiology.  Its
principal contribution lies in the use of the notion of
model as a means of shedding light on some aspects of
the church.

A model is not an equation.  Rather, it is an
heuristic "angle of vision" which organizes our
perception of church in a particular way and sheds light
on one dimension of the mystery which is the Church.  A
model is, then, a point of view which serves to
integrate the various components of our understanding of
the Church.  As with all points of view, one cannot be
totally separated from the other.  Yet there is a
distinct perspective on reality which exists because
one has adopted a given point of view or angle of

vision. In one's personal ecclesiology, especially in one's operative ecclesiology, there is generally a single and specific appreciation of the church which predominates. This appreciation serves to focus, integrate, and organize one's varied insights into the church.

## Models of the Church

1. *The Church as Institution.* This is the notion of the church which dominated Roman Catholic ecclesiology from the Counter-Reformation until the Second Vatican Council. It is frequently associated with the work of Robert Bellarmine (1542-1621) and is the ecclesiology which received juridical form in the 1917 *Codex Juris Canonici.*[3]

This type of ecclesiology defines the Church in terms of its structures and highlights the structures of government as the formal element in society. The "powers" of government are of singular importance in an ecclesiology of this kind. The principal powers and functions of the church are teaching, sanctifying, and governing. All three of these powers are exercised by the governing body. Hence there is a hierarchical concept of authority in the notion of church as institution.

The chief assets of this understanding of church are three. First of all, the theory has strong endorsement in official documents of the (Roman Catholic) church of the past few centuries. Because the approach strongly insists on the element of continuity with Christian origins, the model provides important links between an uncertain present and an esteemed religious past. Finally, the model has served to provide Roman Catholics with a strong sense of identity.

Yet there are weaknesses inherent in the use of the model as a primary mode of understanding the church. It has a relatively weak basis in Scripture and the early history of the church. It has had unfortunate consequences in the Christian life, as it tends to emphasize obedience at the expense of personal charism and responsibility. It frequently inhibits a creative and fruitful theology. Finally it raises serious theological problems and is out of phase with the demands of the times.

2. *The Church as Mystical Communion.* This approach to an understanding of the church is reflected in the writings of Johann Adam Möhler, Yves Congar, Jerome Hamer, and Heribert Mühlen, and is found in Vatican II's *Lumen Gentium.* The conciliar document, the cornerstone of the Vatican II *aggiornamento,* used the biblical images of the People of God and the Body of Christ in order to elucidate the mystery of the church.

From the perspective of this model, the church is a communion of men and women.[4] This communion is primarily an interior reality, but it is also expressed by external bonds of creed, worship, and ecclesiastical fellowship. The bonds of union within the church are primarily the interior graces and gifts of the Spirit, but external bonds of union are recognized as being also important, albeit in subsidiary fashion.

Among the assets of the model are its biblical base, particularly in those passages of the Scriptures which speak of κοινωνία (community) and τὸ σῶμα τοῦ χριστοῦ (the Body of Christ). The model has a foundation in the Catholic theological tradition — such giants of the tradition as Augustine and Aquinas having written on the theme of *communio.* The use of this model helps to revivify spirituality and the life of prayer. Finally, a church understood according to this angle of vision meets some of the human needs acutely experienced by many members of the church today.

Nonetheless this type of ecclesiology suffers from certain weaknesses as well. It leaves some obscurity regarding the relationships between the spiritual and visible dimensions of the church. It tends to exalt and divinize the church beyond its due.[5] Often it fails to give Christians a clear sense of their identity and mission. Finally there is a certain tension between the church as a network of friendly, interpersonal relationships and the church as a mystical communion of grace.

3. *The Church as Sacrament.* Among those who see the church from this angle are Henri deLubac, Karl Rahner, Edward Schillebeeckx, John Paul II[6] and the Fathers of the Second Vatican Council.

From this point of view the church is not only "sign" but "sacrament". Where the church is present as sacrament, there the grace of Christ will not be absent. The church thus becomes an event of grace. Grace impels men and women to prayer, confession, worship, and other acts wherein the church externally realizes its existence.

One of the chief strengths of this ecclesial model is that it relates the idea of church as institution with the idea of church as mystical communion. Another asset of this model is that it gives ample scope to the workings of divine grace beyond the limits of the institutional church, without thereby neglecting the importance of the visible church. It has had the ability of integrating ecclesiology with the other traditional theological themes, especially Christology and sacramentology.

It has been objected that this type of ecclesiology has comparatively little warrant in Scripture, and that the model focuses too much on the external aspects of the church with a corresponding neglect of emphasis upon the mystery of the church.[7] Some of its early formulations were judged to be burdened with a narrow sacramentalism and an insufficient attention to *diakonia* (service) in its vision of the church's mission. Finally it should be mentioned that this model finds little echo in contemporary Protestant ecclesiology.

4. *The Church as Herald.* This is the "kerygmatic" model of the church, attested by Karl Barth, Hans Küng, and Richard McBrien. It sees the church as gathered and formed by the Word of God. The mission of the church is to proclaim that which it has heard, believed, and been commissioned to proclaim. Within this model of ecclesiology the emphasis lies on faith as the principal bond of communion.

This type of ecclesiology has a good biblical foundation in the prophetic tradition of the Old Testament and the letters of Paul. It provides a clear sense of identity and mission for the church, especially for the local church. It is conducive to a spirituality that focuses on God's sovereignty and humankind's infinite distance from him. Hence the virtues of obedience, humility, and conversion are stressed. Finally this model of ecclesiology gives rise to a rich theology of the word.

On the other hand, this model does not sufficiently stress the incarnational aspect of Revelation. It can lead to a discontinuous view of the church, almost as if the church were a series of totally disconnected happenings. Finally, it focuses too

134

exclusively on witness to the neglect of action.

5. *The Church as Servant.* This model of the church is found in the writings of Teilhard de Chardin, Dietrich Bonhoeffer, and many liberation theologians.[8] It appeared in a 1966 pastoral letter of Richard Cardinal Cushing.[9] This is the "diaconal" model of ecclesiology which underscores the special competence of the church to keep alive the hopes and aspirations of men and women for the kingdom of God and its values. The church offers guidance and prophetic criticism; it promotes the mutual reconciliation of human beings, and initiates them in various ways into the kingdom of God.

The strongest claim to acceptance of this model lies in the new situation in which the church presently finds itself. Its greatest weakness is that it lacks a clear biblical basis. Moreover there is the problem of the nature of the relationship between the church and the kingdom of God.

### An Evaluation

In his evaluation of the models,[10] Dulles has identified seven useful criteria: (1) basis in Scripture; (2) basis in Christian tradition; (3) capacity to give church members a sense of their corporate identity and mission; (4) the tendency to foster the virtues and values generally admired by Christians; (5) correspondence with the religious experience of men today; (6) theological fruitfulness; and (7) fruitfulness in enabling church members to relate successfully to those outside their own group. Upon assessment it will be seen that the basic assertions by each of these five ecclesiological types are valid, yet each one of the types can lead to a serious imbalance and distortion.

1. *The Church as Institution.*
   (+) The church must be a structured community, It must remain the type of institution that Christ instituted, including the pastoral office.
   (-) The tendency to become rigid, doctrinaire, conformist.

2. *The Church as Mystical Communion.*
   (+) The church is united to God by grace. In the strength of that grace its members must lovingly be united to one another.

135

(-) An unhealthy enthusiasm. Perhaps, community for community's sake, without sufficient attention to the *raison d'être* of the community which is the church.

3. *The Church as Sacrament.*
   (+) In its visible aspects the church ought to be a sign of the continuing vitality of the grace of Christ, and of the redemption which he has promised.

   (-) This model of ecclesiology can lead to a "sterile estheticism and to an almost narcicisstic self-contemplation."[11]

4. *The Church as Herald.*
   (+) This model accentuates the necessity for the church to continue to herald the Gospel and to move men and women to put their faith in Jesus as Lord and Savior.
   (-) This model runs the risk of falling into the exaggerations of the biblicists and fundamentalist sects.

5. *The Church as Servant.*
   (+) This point of view points up the urgency of making the church contribute to the transformation of the secular life, and of impregnating human life as a whole with the values of the kingdom of God.
   (-) This perspective easily gives the impression that final salvation is to be found within history. It could easily lead the church into an uncritical acceptance of secular values.[12]

   In point of fact each of the five models is inadequate to the reality to which it points. We must therefore harmonize the different models in such a way that their differences become complementary rather than mutually repugnant. Each of these models then must be criticized in the light of all the others. When this is done, it becomes apparent that one of the models cannot be taken as primary, writes Dulles. The model, of the five, which cannot be primary is the institutional model.[13]

To each of these models of church corresponds a model of ministry.[14] These models of ministry reflect the particular "angles of vision" at work in the various models of the church.

(1) To the church as institution corresponds a ministry of organizing. It is a juridical model of ministry. It leads to a ministry which is in accordance with the canons of the Code, one which consists largely in the fulfillment of directives which come from "on high". This form of ministry consists of the exercise of powers which were conferred through a valid and licit ordination.

Positively, this form of ministry is necessary in that without the ministry of organizing the church would be a chaotic band of "semi-like minded" individuals. Negatively, this type of ministry gives rise to clericalism, in which ministry is the privilege of a few.

(2) To the church as community corresponds the ministry of pastoral care. Ministry is considered to be a matter of fostering fellowship among members of the community.

Positively, this form of ministry incorporates a vision of shared responsibility. Negatively, a communitarian ecclesiology tends to weaken the cultic or mystical dimensions of ministry. It can lead to a search for the perfect community. It can lead the minister to want community "for community's sake", with little attention to organization and/or proclamation of the Gospel.

(3) To the church as sacrament corresponds the ministry of celebration. Ministry is seen as a mediation between God and humankind, which functions primarily in the sacramental order. This model of ministry is "priestly" in both the narrow and the broad sense. It is useful for recovering the liturgical and spiritual development of every ministry in the church.

Positively, this model of ministry is significant in that it calls to mind that in every ministry God is made present through the symbol which is the minister. For example, the deacon incarnates, in symbolic fashion, the church's mission of service (*diakonia*). Negatively,

137

the minister can become a surrogate for the community. This can conceivably lead to the development of a caste system within the church. For example, the experience of the restoration of the permanent diaconate in the United States[15] offers many examples of the defects inherent in the "sacramentalization" of ministry.

(4) To the church as herald corresponds a ministry of preaching and teaching. The minister is the one who articulates in evocative language the faith experience of the community and calls the community to judgment on the basis of its biblical roots.

Positively, this model of ministry provides a solid theological basis for the Christian life and ministry. Negatively, ministry is easily reducible to the production of the "word event". An emphasis upon the competence of the minister for preaching and teaching can lead to a form of "neo-gnosticism".

(5) Finally, to the church as Servant corresponds a ministry of healing. The minister is the one who binds up the wounds of society as a whole. According to most authors, this form of ministry would involve political activity.

Positively, this understanding of ministry conveys an enthusiastic sense of mission. It overcomes the sterility of an inward-directed communitarianism or the narcissism of an exclusively ritualistic understanding of ministry. Negatively, this approach can lead to an exaggerated secularism or professionalism.

In an evaluation of the "models of ministry", George Weigel has taken a cue from Milton Mayeroff's *On Caring*[16] to offer a view of ministry as caring, as "helping the other to grow."[17] In fact, a comprehensive view of ministry is as necessary as a comprehensive view of the church. The strengths of one model of ministry should serve as a critique of the other models of ministry. Since one's view of the church is the context within which ministry is exercised, the only radically deficient view of ministry is a ministry of organizing which does not proceed beyond the organization to the *raison d'être* of the organization. Nonetheless the espousal of a ministry of service without some significant expression of the explicit proclamation of the Gospel would seem quickly to lose its ability to "signify" the church.

*Example 1: Preaching.*

Preaching is a characteristic form of ministry. As such it is a sign of the church. The church is the referent of one's preaching.

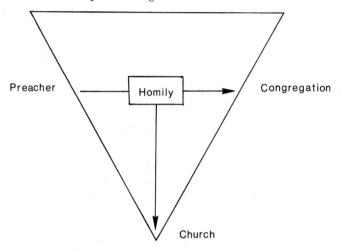

Yet the preacher should ask himself about the "operative ecclesiology" of his or her preaching.[18] What is the model of church which is the effective referent of that preaching?

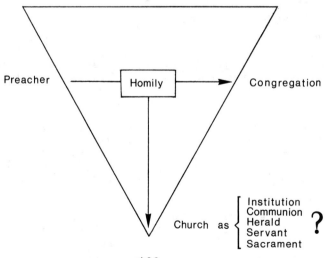

To the institutional model of church corresponds one rather specific type of preaching. For the institutional model of church it is vitally important that all the tests of membership be visible, that is to say, juridically applicable. Consequently there will be an emphasis on the valid, licit, and worthy reception of the sacraments in preaching which proceeds from an operative institutional model of ecclesiology. Sermons consistent with this model will tend to be moralizing since it is important that the church be built up as a "holiness community", the "perfect" society.

Different homiletic emphases will appear in preaching that reflect the other models of church. The theme of sharing in the life of God through Jesus and the Spirit will be a feature of homilies that correspond to the communion model of church. Such homilies will dwell on the importance of community, participation, sharing, and building one another up. To the church as sacrament corresponds a homiletic emphasis on celebration. The liturgy itself will be the center of attention in many of the sermons which correspond to this ecclesiology.

Preaching that is Scripturally based and is permeated with references to the Scriptures is a feature of homilies which cohere with a kerygmatic ecclesiology. The call to conversion and the call to witness are themes which will occur with some frequency. In sermons that reflect a servant ecclesiology "love your neighbor" echoes almost as a refrain. Service and social justice will be the principal homiletic themes motivated by this type of ecclesiology.

That the sermon corresponds to an operative ecclesiology was recently confirmed by a conversation among myself, a local pastor, and several deacons. Part of the conversation bore on the fact that the theme of love was no longer as dominant a feature of homilies preached to American congregations as it had been in the mid-seventies. Further reflection brought out the realization that the relatively lesser frequency of the homiletic theme was concomitant with a change in the practical posture of the church. The church has become more introspective and less concerned with social causes than it had been just a few years ago.

*Example 2: the Prayer of the Minister.*
When a minister asks why he or she prays or for whom is the prayer offered, the response will frequently point to an operative ecclesiology.

An institutional ecclesiology is reflected in prayer that is dictated by the canons of the code or by diocesan policy. The minister's life of prayer will feature the breviary and the stipulated yearly retreat. A confirmation of the correspondence between this mode of prayer and ecclesiology can be found in the rejection of the Latin breviary as a form of prayer by many Roman Catholic priests in the days after Second Vatican Council. As they rejected, at least to some degree, the institutional elements of the church, so they abandoned the breviary as a viable form of prayer.

To the model of church as community corresponds a prayer life that features prayer with and for others. On the part of a priest, this ecclesiology almost demands prayer among the group of priests living together in a rectory. It will call forth shared prayer within the diocesan presbyterate. It will seek out prayer with parishioners and support the existence of prayer groups, with the vigorous participation in these groups of both clerics and laity.

To the church as sacrament corresponds a focus on liturgical prayer. Indeed as the sacramental model of the church is an integrating model (a paradigm), so liturgical prayer has an integrating function. To the church as herald corresponds an emphasis on the visibility of prayer. Praying the Scriptures is a feature of a life of prayer that corresponds to the church as herald.

Finally, a certain attitude toward prayer would be typical of those whose ministry operates from a servant model of ecclesiology. "My life (and/or work) is a prayer" is often the slogan of those who see the church principally as a servant. When formal prayer is a feature of their lives, this prayer often is a prayer of petition for those outside the church. It is a prayer for the poor and others who are in need. It is a prayer for social justice. Oftentimes prayer will be offered within the context of a political or social demonstration. According to the ITT, this type of prayer would reflect a servant church in this manner:

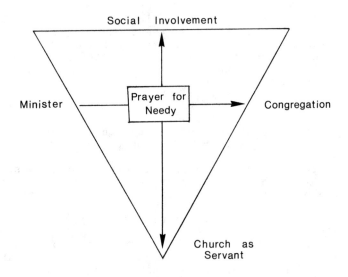

Social Involvement

Minister

Prayer for Needy

Congregation

Church as Servant

*Example 3:  Priorities in the Life of a Minister.*
One can determine one's operative priorities
according to the way one spends time.   We find time
for the things we consider to be valuable.  We find time
for the activities that truly interest us.   Thus a
realistic assessment of one's time commitment is
revelatory of one's operative ecclesiology.

Vast amounts of time devoted to administration or
the implementation of policies and programs dictated by
diocesan (or other authoritative) directives reflect an
institutional model of ecclesiology.  When one's
priorities include getting annual reports in on time,
but when one does not spend a realistic amount of time
on the preparation (both proximate and remote) of one's
homilies, an observer should conclude that the operative
model of church is the institutional one.

When community is the operative model of church,
then parish life, parish visitation, and non-pragmatic
("useless"[19]) activities will be a prominent part of
one's ministerial life.  When the sacramental model of
church provides the context of one's ministry, time,
energy, and even money will be committed to the building
up of a parish as a liturgically oriented community.
The participation of the parishioners in the various
liturgical capacities (lectors, Eucharistic ministers,
host families, and so forth) will be considered a
priority.  Sacramental programs will be instituted, and

care will be taken that lectors and acolytes are properly prepared for their task.

When herald is the operative model of one's ecclesiology, then witness on behalf of "gospel" values will be an important feature of one's ministerial life. Classes in adult education (Bible classes especially) will be seen as a priority within one's parish. The preparation of homilies will be an important feature of one's ministerial life. In contrast, when the church as servant is the operative model of ecclesiology, community organization will be featured. Issues of peace and justice — demonstrations, workshops, political involvement, monetary support, and so forth — will dominate one's ministerial life.

*Example 4: Papal Visits.*
Pope John Paul II has continued the practice inaugurated by his predecessor, Pope Paul VI, of visiting different nations. One can reflect on the style of these visits. What type of church do they signify?

Newspaper reports of the papal visit to Brazil in July, 1980, featured such stories as these:

"The pope arrived in the industrial city of Belo Horizonte and made a 12-mile (20 km) ride in an open-air vehicle to the Mass site. A Brazilian television network estimated the crowd at more than 500,000, although no official figures were available.

"The crowd chanted 'Hey, hey, hey John Paul is our king.' Others held up signs that said 'I love you.'..."[20]

"Porto Alegre, Brazil (AP)... interrupted repeatedly by chants of more than 100 thousand people wildly waving yellow and white Vatican flags and chanting 'The pope is our king.' John Paul said that the mass media has bred passivity and emotionalism, manipulation and, consequently, evasion and hedonism."[21]

"Curitiba, Brazil, July 6... About 150,000 people, most of them waving white and yellow Vatican flags, were waiting for the pope at the main square of Curitiba, the capital of southern Brazil's rich Parana state. But after he arrived in his limosine, the crowd swelled impressively, building up to a more than half a million in the space of ten minutes."[22]

The crowd's reaction to the pope's visit to Brazil

143

was expressed in their waving of flags and chanting a
royal cry.  Along the syntactic axis, these symbols are
clearly associated with royalty.  They manifest an
appreciation of the papal visit as that of a monarch.
From the standpoint of ecclesiological reflection, the
papal visit was perceived as an expression of a
monarchical presence, that is as a form of ministerial
presence which is a symbol of the church as institution.

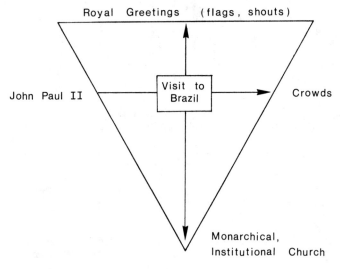

That this was in fact the dominant significance of
the visit is confirmed by the fact that the National
Conference of Brazilian Bishops wanted the pope to first
appear on July 9 in Fortaleza, a site located in the
poor, problem-ridden northeast corner of Brazil, the
city in which the Eucharistic Congress was held.  The
Vatican view was that the Pontiff's first stop should be
in Brasilia, the nation's capital.  While there may have
been diplomatic reasons for the choice of Brasilia over
Fortaleza as the site of the first pontifical appearance
in Brazil, the choice syntactically coheres with the
reaction of the crowds in Belo Horizaonte, Porto Alegre,
and Curitiba as an indication that the visits were
perceived in political terms.  They manifestly
"signified" an institutional model of church.

Further reflection along the syntactic axis would
lead one to associate the papal visit to Brazil with
other papal visits, for example, John Paul's visit to
the United States in October, 1979.  A group of students

from a Catholic university were asked what they thought
of the papal visit.  To a person, they were singularly
impressed by his personal charisma.  When they were
asked to judge the acceptability of twenty statements of
church teaching taken from among the pope's seventy-two
addresses in the United States,[23] they found that
only two were acceptable.

This twofold  reaction indicates the acceptance of
the person, but not of the teacher.  The significance of
this ambivalent reaction can be elucidated by further
use of the ITT.

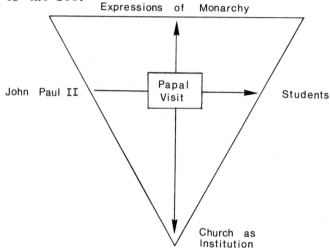

Along the syntactic axis, the pope's visit is associated
with expressions of royalty.  Today, given the
constitutional monarchies with which most westerners are
familiar, the royal "sign system" implies a monarchy
with which symbolism (and heritage), but not real power
is associated.  It is appropriate to treat a monarch
with awe and reverence; it is not expected that the
monarch should exercise real power over one's life.

That the style of papal leadership is that of the
institutional type is confirmed by the fact that during
the 1979 meeting of the USCC/NCCB, twenty-seven bishops
were recorded as being in favor of adding to the
official letter of thanks of the American hierarchy to
the pope a request that the pope make provisions for
listening to the bishops of the country during his visit
to the Unites States.  The reaction of these students

145

and of this small group of bishops, though episodic, confirm that the style of the pontifical visit does not reflect the church as community, sacrament, or herald — still less that of servant — but an institutional model of church.

That this indeed is John Paul II's style of church leadership was confirmed by a *Time* magazine article which commented upon the choice of Cardinal Ratzinger as the new Prefect of the Congregation for the Doctrine of the Faith and the appointment of Fr. Paolo Dezza as his personal delegate to direct the Society of Jesus.[25] Couched in the language of journalism the article concluded: "John Paul, adds one unhappy Vatican observer, 'really wants to see a kind of highly organized church with the Pope at the top, bishops underneath, and clergy beneath them — all tidy-like.'"[26] Indeed it is clear that John Paul II has opted for the institutional model of ecclesiology. His actions are so many signs that this indeed his real choice.

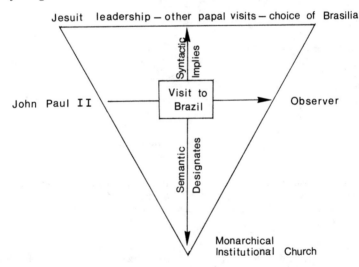

*A Brief Reflection*

In each of these four examples, we have been involved in the analytic part of theological reflection. We are seeking to understand the meaning of the message about the church that is being sent by various forms of ministerial activity. Diagnosis must procede a critique. It is only after one has understood an experience, that one should proceed to a judgment about

146

it. The reflection on John Paul's style of
pontificating is not intended to be judgmental; it is
meant only to clarify what his style really is. The
reflection was an exercise in diagnosis. It is only
after one has determined an operative ecclesiology that
one should presume to judge it.

Avery Dulles used the seven criteria cited above[27]
in an attempt to offer a critique of the five models of
ecclesiology which he discerned and characterized.
Subsequently he reflected that: "One of the five models
... cannot be properly taken as primary — and this is
the institutional model. Of their very nature,...
institutions are subordinate to persons, structures are
subordinate to life. 'The Sabbath was made for man, not
man for the Sabbath' (Mk 2:27). Without calling into
question the value and importance of institutions, one
may feel that this value does not properly appear unless
it can be seen that the structure effectively helps to
make the Church a community of grace, a sacrament of
Christ, a herald of salvation, and a servant of
mankind."[28]

Dulles judges that an institutional model of
ecclesiology should not be one's operative model of
church in a primary way. For purpose of the present
systematic analysis of a model of theological reflection
such a judgment can be temporarily suspended. In
chapters ten and eleven we will be dealing with aspects
of the theological reflection process that pertain to
the judgment one should bring to bear upon one's
ministry and the ministerial church as one seeks to know
and take responsibility for ministry itself. Thus we
can move from ecclesiology as a framework of theological
reflection to Christology.

1. See T. Johannes van Bavel, "What Kind of Church Do You Want? The Breadth of Augustine's Ecclesiology," *Louvain Studies* 7 (1978-1979) 147-171.

2. Avery Dulles, *Models of the Church. A Critical Assessment of the Church in All its Aspects* (Garden City: Doubleday, 1974).

3. The 1983 *Codex* attempted to incorporate other ecclesiological notions according to Vatican Council II's *Lumen Gentium*. On this point, see, for example, James H. Provost, "The Revised Code: A New Way of Thinking for Church and about Priests," *Louvain Studies* 9 (1982-1983) 226-235. Elements of the ecclesiology present in the 1917 code apparently continue, however, to predominate in the new code. It is obvious, of course, that institutional elements would receive preponderant emphasis in a code of law. The ecclesiological tension in the new code was described by Provost as follows: "A first expression of... new thinking is in the whole understanding of the church which is reflected in the Code. The 1917 Code clearly addressed the church as a monarchy, a religious government with institutions stretching from the universal to the most local neighborhood levels. The revised Code attempts to take seriously the sense of church as a communion, a bonding together of people in the Lord and with one another at various levels of their church experience. Many of the structures of the old Code are still here, but the attempt has been made to address them in a new context" ("The Revised Code: A Promising Vintage," *America* 148 (1983) 85-88, p. 87).

4. See Barbara Glendon, "Models of Community," *Review for Religious* 38 (1979) 206-216.

5. See Charles Morris who wrote that "Signs normally take the place of objects they designate only to a limited extent; but if for various reasons interests cannot be satisfied in the objects themselves, the signs come more and more to take the place of the object" (C. W. Morris, *art. cit.*, p. 120). While the community of the church may tend to take the place of the communion of the church, it is also true that one of the practical liabilities of the institutional model of ecclesiology is that it tends to replace the realities of grace with the institutional elements of the church — elements which are but a sign and means of grace-filled

realities.

6. See above, p. 33, n. 33.

7. Dulles has cited Jerome Hamer, presently the
number 2 man in the Congregation for the Doctrine
of the Faith, as one theologian who has voiced this
criticism. He offers Richard McBrien as an example
of one who has criticized the sacramental model of
ecclesiology on the basis of its lesser emphasis
upon the diaconal aspects of the mission of the
church. See A. Dulles, *op. cit.*, p. 69.

8. Cf. Donald W. Shriver, "Gospel Message and Social
Witness: The Church as a Form of Evangelism,"
*Perkins Journal* 35 (1981) 3-11.

9. Richard Cushing, *The Servant Church* (Boston:
Daughters of St. Paul, 1966).

10. See Chapter XII, "The Evaluation of Models, in
*Models of the Church*, pp. 179-192.

11. A. Dulles, *op. cit.*, p. 184.

12. See U. T. Holmes, *art. cit.*, p. 132.

13. A. Dulles, *op. cit.*, p. 187.

14. See George S. Weigel, Jr., "Ministering as Caring,"
*Chicago Studies* 16 (1977) 219-235.

15. Approximately one third of the permanent deacons
ordained in the Roman Catholic church reside in the
U.S. In the wake of the experience a number of
dioceses are presently reconsidering ordination to
the permanent diaconate in the context of broader
ministerial programs. Using the "trial and error"
method, these diocese have discovered what many
African bishops suspected at the time of the
Council. Many of these were opposed to the
restoration of the permanent diaconate less it
clericalize other practicable forms of ministry,
particularly the ministry of the catechist.

16. Milton Mayeroff, *On Caring*, ed. by Ruth N. Anshen
(New York: Harper & Row, 1971).

17. See G. S. Weigel, *art. cit.*, pp. 224-235.

18. It is difficult to speak of one's operative

ecclesiology on the basis of an analysis of a single sermon. In my judgement one might take an analysis of the group of sermons delivered over a six-month period as a "litmus test" experience.

19. The Germans often distinguish society (*Gesellschaft*) from the community (*Gemeinschaft*). Society and associations are distinguished by a practical purpose; communities have their *raison d'être* within themselves. They are not goal or purpose oriented. The family is the paradigm of *Gemeinschaft*. Within a family, time together is important — not so that the members of the family can *do* something together, but so that they can *be* together. Analogously, a vision of church as communion/community dictates that its minister be involved in activities whose principal purpose is simply that of mutual presence, of "being with".

20. *International Herald Tribune*, July 2, 1980, p. 1.

21. *Stars and Stripes*, July 6, 1980.

22. *International Herald Tribune*, July 7, 1980.

23. At the time of the inquiry the students were, in fact, unaware that the doctrinal statements to be judged were specifically taken from the Pope's American addresses.

24. See also Ann Scurfield, "A question of orthodoxy," *The Tablet* 236 (1982) 984-986.

25. See also John F. X. Harriott, "The Pope and the Jesuits," *The Tablet* 235 (1981) 1110; "Fr Dezza's mission," *The Tablet* 235 (1981) 1150-1151.

26. "Hardening the Papal Lineup. John Paul picks a German Cardinal as his doctrinal watchdog," *Time* (December 14, 1981) p. 38.

27. See above, p. 135.

28. A. Dulles, *op. cit.*, p. 187.

# Chapter Ten

The Christological Model

*How Do We See Jesus?*

In *Models of Jesus*,[1] John O'Grady has developed a
new approach to Christology.[2] He distinguished half a
dozen different "Models of Jesus."

*Models of Jesus*

*1. The Incarnation of the Second Person of the Blessed
Trinity.* According to the Council of Chalcedon (451),
"Our Lord Jesus Christ is one and the same Son, the same
perfect in Godhead, the same perfect in manhood, truly
God and truly Man."[3] The model of Christology which
results from theological elaboration upon the
Chalcedonian definition is one which situates
Christology within an elaborated doctrine of the
Trinity. Consequently one can arrive at certain
conclusions about the life and death, the mission and
ministry of Jesus.

The incarnational model of Christology is that
found in classical Western Christology.[4] This model has
important theological implications. For example, it
leads one to raise the question of the purpose of the
Incarnation. If the Second Person of the Trinity pre-
existed creation, why did he enter into the created
sphere? The dogma of virginal conception is seen to be
rather important since "the model of Jesus as the Second
Person of the Blessed Trinity gives support to the
doctrine of the virginal conception just as the dogma of
the virginal conception supports the belief that Jesus
is the Second Person of the Blessed Trinity."[5] Jesus is
free from sin and immune from temptation. Typically,
two kinds of knowledge, corresponding to the two natures
of the Second Person, are attributed to Jesus — a divine
knowledge, and a human, experiential, knowledge.
Finally, the Resurrection is seen as (but) the greatest
miracle of Jesus.[6] Indeed, the Resurrection did not
figure prominently in those Christologies which focused
especially on the Second Person of the Trinity.

Among the strengths of this model are its clarity
and the fact that it has been the traditional, and
operative, model of Christology in the church for
centuries. It has a conciliar basis. Moreover, the
approach is clearly theandric, in that the divinity of
Jesus is preserved and highlighted. Finally, the model
is theologically useful. A fair amount of theological
elaboration has been developed on the basis of an
incarnational approach to Christology.

On the other hand, however, the model has only a
meager basis in Scripture.[7] Secondly, the model tends
to eclipse the meaning of the humanity of Jesus. Jesus'
humanity is reduced to a kind of instrument for the
divinity. Thirdly, the model is somewhat constrictive
with regards to the development of theology. The self-
assured character of one's Christological statements
tends to impose itself on other areas of theology and
tends to inhibit the breaking of new theological ground.
Fourthly, "this model is detrimental to Christian piety,
since it can easily create a situation in which the
ordinary believer cannot identify with Jesus."[8] Indeed,
in this respect, it has been observed that much of the
recent emphasis on Marian piety in Roman Catholicism was
the counterpart of the distancing of Jesus from the life
of the ordinary believer. Finally, this approach to
Christology is not in tune with current developments in
theology and the life of the church. It is difficult to
interpret the Christ of Chalcedon (and its dependent
tradition) according to the categories of recent
philosophy. Moreover, there would seem to be some
distance between this approach and both the aspirations
and the anguish of many contemporary Christians.

2. *The Mythological Jesus.* This model came to the
surface in the writings of many searchers during the
time of the Quest of the Historical Jesus, especially
in the writings of David Friedrich Strauss.[9] Most
recently it has been popularized in Great Britain in
such works as John A. T. Robinson's *Honest to God*[10] and
*The Myth of God Incarnate*,[11] the collected reflections
of several Anglican divines. Bultmann's kerygmatic
Christology[12] can also be brought under the umbrella of
the mythological model. For Bultmann Christ is the
event of salvation, but this does not necessarily
include the historical Jesus.

Each of the authors whose approach to Christology
can be understood as mythological uses the notion of
myth in his or her own fashion. For Bultmann, myth is a
way of presenting things so that the other world becomes

worldly, the divine is seen in the human. What is communicated in myth is often much more than can be communicated in strictly scientific or historical language. Myth is an interpretive language, which functions by means of analogy with human activity. Subsequently one can study the environment in which myth arose in an effort to ascertain how Jesus was interpreted.[13]

Among the assets of the mythological model are that it affirms the close relationship between Christianity and the environment from which it arose. Secondly, it serves as a reminder that there are some elements of Christology that should not be taken as absolutes. Some aspects of Christology are indeed time and culture conditioned. Thirdly, the mythological approach allows one to move from a theoretical understanding of Jesus to an existential one. Finally, the mythological model allows the theologian a fair amount of freedom for inquiry by releasing dogma from its rigidity.

The mythological model suffers, however, from serious liabilities. First of all, it divorces the Christ of faith almost completely from the historical Jesus. For Bultmann it was simply necessary to affirm that Jesus existed in order that there be a Christ of faith. Secondly, Christianity itself is relativized to a large extent by the mythological model. There are no particular contours which can be ascribed to Christianity. Thirdly, this model is so freeing that it removes any sense of stability and thereby can be dangerous for the theological endeavor. Finally, the model calls into question the very truth of Christianity.

3. *The Ethical Liberator.* This is the model of Christology found to be most congenial by the proponents of liberation theology. To a large degree liberation theology has been criticized, and justly, for failing to provide a theological base for its "theologizing". The works of Jan Sobrino and Leonardo Boff on Christology[14] have sought to provide such a base.

The popularity of this type of Christology for the oppressed Christians of Latin America is due to the similarity between the situation of the churches in Latin America and the situation in which Jesus himself lived, as this is perceived by some theologians. The Ethical Liberator type of Christology capitalizes on an idea emphasized by many New Testament scholars, namely

153

that Christology did not arise from the world of academia, rather it developed around two poles, the historical Jesus and the concrete situation of the churches.

Certain common traits arise in the works of the liberation theologians, for whom the kingdom of God is a most powerful symbol. The symbol points to the reversal of the old order. Within this perspective Jesus is seen as a liberator, and a nonconformist. The salvation which he came to bring, construed largely in political terms, was both universal and individual. Thus the emphasis in liberation theology is not on future, universal salvation; it is on present, individual liberation. With this vision of Jesus, the proponents of liberation theology turn their attention to tactics, both those of Jesus and those of the liberation theology movement itself. For them, transformation takes place through politics, struggle, and suffering.

Among the assets of this approach is that it corresponds to a need felt by groups of Christians, especially those in Latin America, where a large percentage of the Catholic Christian population of the world is presently concentrated, but also those oppressed Christian groups in other parts of the world, for example the Philippines and South Africa. Secondly, the model highlights the call for social justice which is an easily overshadowed aspect of the Gospel. Thirdly, the model is relevant to anyone who is seeking freedom and liberation within an oppressive society. Fourthly, the model is pertinent to an understanding of the church and its structures. Finally, the model has implications for other aspects of theology. For example, it would abide a great amount of freedom with regards to sexual ethics, and would require the church to allow a greater measure of freedom to those whose theological opinions are not in consort with traditional theological positions.

On the other hand, there are also drawbacks to this type of an approach to Christology. First of all, liberation theologians tend to make Jesus a revolutionary and to lose sight of the Christian belief that professes him to be the Son of God.[15] Secondly, this approach suffers from a certain reductionism, particularly of a political and social nature. Thirdly, the tactics which result can be misunderstood, particularly if the means become an end, violence is raised to the level of a principle, and a Marxist humanism is identified with Christianity. Fourthly, the

model does not sufficiently come to grips with the
problem of evil in the world and in every individual.
In practice, the liberators frequently become
oppressors. Finally, there is some ambiguity as to how
liberation can be described empirically. Just what does
it mean to be liberated?

4. *The Human Face of God.* This model is a type of that
Christology "from below" which has characterized so much
contemporary Christological reflection. Christology
from below begins with the Jesus of history, a man like
us in all things except sin, who stands out from the
rest of the human race by his proclamation of, and
commitment to, the kingdom of God. His life of
dedicated service of others led him to the cross, from
which God raised him up and exalted him. This was the
emphasis of the Synoptic Gospels.[16] The Christology
which focuses on Jesus as the human face of God is
principally represented by the works of the Dutch trio,[17]
Schoonenberg,[18] Hulsbosch,[19] and Schillebeeckx.[20] It is
also reflected in the writings of two of the German
"wonder children"[21] at the Second Vatican Council, Hans
Küng and Karl Rahner.

Besides enjoying congeniality with the Synoptic
images of Jesus, this model is the modern counterpart of
the theological reflection of the school of Antioch
which emphasized the humanity of Jesus. This human face
of God approach develops Christology within the context
of anthropology.[22] The model does not deny the
Chalcedonian faith; rather it places emphasis upon the
"truly man" formula of the conciliar definition. The
model, moreover, is one which allows some openness to
the process theology[23] proposed by many proponents of
philosophical theology, particularly in North America.

Underlying this approach to Christology is the
traditional Christian notion that man is created in the
image of God (Gen 1:27). If this is so, there is no
need to find in Jesus the "ideal man". Rather one can
take the human Jesus and relate his experience to all
human experiences. His human experience included a
strong religious experience, in which we can discern
both the experience of intimacy with God (Jesus' *Abba*
prayer)[24] and a keen sense of his dependency on God.
Jesus, moreover, had both a unique sense of his own
goodness and a remarkable ability to express the power
of goodness. In him there was not to be found that
evil-provoked division which is called sin in
theological language.

Jesus had a definite sense of purpose as O'Grady explained: "His actions, his words, even his basic attitude toward human life seemed to have its roots within. Jesus lived by transferring the epicenter of his life to God, to Abba, and thus the externals always expressed the internal principle. This does not mean that he found his center of existence outside of himself; rather he discovered his center was his relationship to God and thus he could live a harmonious life in which the outward expression flowed from an inner conviction."[25]

The two poles of his existence — his relationship to God, and the way he expressed this relationship in life — marked his attitudes and activities. These bore the expression of the divine. They remained human but through them the divine was transparent, to wit, "The attitudes displayed by Jesus in his personal concern for the poor, the compassion he offered to those who were the outcasts of society, the kindness he manifested to sinners, to widows, to children, to his disciples and friends — all these are human dimensions of his personality, but they also express God's concerns."[26]

The advantages of such a model of Christology are apparent. First of all, the model emphasizes the totality of Jesus of Nazareth as the expression and revelation of God. Moreover it relates Jesus to the ordinary experience of human life. With this model, no false dichotomy exists between the human and the divine.[27] This model also restores a sense of balance to Christianity, which, in times past, too often emphasized the spiritual to the disadvantage of the material. It is a model which avoids excessive concentration upon future salvation at the expense of the present moment of salvation. Finally, the model has substantial scriptural warrants and important pastoral implications.

Yet there are possible weaknesses, the greatest of which is that "the signified can be lost in the sign."[28] There is some danger that the divine will be lost from sight. In addition, there is the possibility that the afterlife will be overlooked. In evaluating the model one must also take into account that the theory which is not built on a sound philosophical foundation will soon collapse. Finally, the danger of pantheism[29] looms large in the background of this model.

5. *The Man for Others*. This type of Christology is represented by the writings of Dietrich Bonhoeffer.[30]

It was popularized in the Anglo-Saxon world by Bishop
John A. T. Robinson.[31]  It is a Christology which sees
Jesus as the center of history and at the border of
one's personal existence insofar as Jesus *both* fulfills
and destroys all human expectations and hopes. Jesus is
to be understood as the presence of God among people.
His humiliation and incarnation arc not separable into
two moments; rather they must *both* be predicated on the
Incarnate One. By following Jesus' example, one will
discover the true meaning of human experience.

The strengths of this approach to Christology are,
first of all, that it brings the gospel and the example
of Jesus to bear upon the personal lives of men and
women. The model puts the present moment and Christian
ethics into proper perspective. It responds to people's
questions about the meaning of human existence.
Moreover the approach accords proportionate weight to
the presentation of Jesus in the Scriptures. Finally,
it serves well the contemporary interest in social
concerns.

On the other hand, the weaknesses of the model are
also apparent. Those who have organized their
Christology around this model have tended to neglect the
long christological tradition of the church. While the
model admittedly focuses on the biblical model of Jesus
as Servant, it tends to overlook other biblical models
of Jesus. In the practical order, the use of the model
tends to overlook the fact that while Christians must be
concerned with the poor and the dispossessed,
Christianity itself does not have a battery of ready
answers with which to solve the problems of the poor.
Moreover, the model tends to obscure the meaning and
importance of the institutional church.

6. *Personal Savior.* This is the model of Jesus which
permeates the faith expression of charismatics and
pentecostalists. It takes its point of departure from
the biblical doctrine of redemption and from the New
Testament description of Jesus as Savior.[32]  Salvation
is generally considered to be an individual experience
and Jesus is thought to be concerned principally with
the healing of the soul, the spiritual dimension of
human life. Jesus saved people from sin and helped them
to overcome concupiscence. Through baptism in the
Spirit one is saved, but salvation is not limited to the
salvation of the soul. Thus healing of the body, mind,
and spirit is very much central to the "evangelical"
idea of salvation. Those who have experienced Jesus as
their savior are generally enthusiastically committed —

both to preaching the message of salvation, and to the community of those who have been "born again".

Among the advantages of this Christological model are its wholistic notion of salvation, which is fully in accord with the Scriptures. It elicits a personal faith commitment together with a strong sense of the community of believers. It conveys a sense of personal well-being to believers and impels them into mission. When one is united to Jesus, nothing is impossible.

Nevertheless there are liabilities which rise to the surface upon analysis. There is a neglect of some aspects of the New Testament portrayal of Jesus, especially of those which point to him as the Transcendent One. Uncritically accepted, the model leads to elitism within the church, and exaggerated emphasis upon the "now".[33] Generally this approach to Christology is accompanied by a fundamentalistic interpretation of the Scriptures. With regards to its ecclesiological implications, the model tends to obscure the real differences that separate the churches from each other, to downplay the institutional elements of the church, and to minimize the significance of the other sacraments (including Eucharist) because of the singular importance of "baptism".

### Evaluation

While recognizing that each of the six models offers some valid insights into the question, "Who is Jesus?", O'Grady has attempted to offer an evaluation of the models.[34] Two levels of evaluation can be discerned. On the one hand is the general acceptability of the model in terms of criteria which he has described. This is clearly the stated agenda in his evaluation of the models. The implicit agenda is the search for a model which has paradigmatic value, that is for a model which is able to integrate a great number of elements of Christological reflection in a manner that is theologically useful and pastorally effective.

In his quest for guidelines on the basis of which he might evaluate each of the six models, O'Grady has identified seven criteria: (1) a firm basis in Scripture; (2) compatibility with Christian tradition; (3) a capacity to help Christians in their efforts to believe in Jesus; (4) a capacity to direct believers to fulfill their mission as members of the church. A

pastorally effective model is one which will enable
believing Christians to employ the charismatic gifts
which are their own. (5) correspondence with the
Christian religious experience today. A theologically
feasible model should correspond to the needs of
Christian piety. (6) theological fruitfulness. A
theologically useful model should provide a foundation
for further theological elaboration and serve as an
integrating element in a theological synthesis. (7) the
ability to foster a good sense of Christian
anthropology.[35] An acceptable Christological model
would help to identify the Christian self-image and
enable Christians to live a fully human life.

1. *The Second Person of the Trinity.*
   (+) The Incarnational model is deeply rooted in
   conciliar, magisterial, and theological
   tradition. It has provided a base for further
   theological reflection, especially in the area
   of ecclesiology.
   (-) The model enjoys little direct Scriptural
   support and encourages a distorted Christian
   anthropology, by fostering a poor appreciation
   of human sexuality and placing salvation almost
   exclusively in the transcendent sphere.

2. *The Mythological Jesus.*
   (+) The mythological model has some foundation in
   Scripture, particularly insofar as mythological
   elements have been utilized to interpret the
   Jesus event, for example in the Matthean and
   Lukan Infancy narratives, and in the use of
   Gnostic Hymn traditions in the Pauline and
   Johannine corpora. Its greatest asset would be
   in the freedom which it accords to the theological
   inquirer.
   (-) The model is weak insofar as it denigrates the
   specificity, indeed the identity, of
   Christianity. Moreover, it appears as if the
   divine is only another way of being human.

3. *The Ethical Liberator.*
   (+) This model has a firm foundation in Scripture.
   It has been found useful for much recent
   theologizing, from the Social Gospel of the
   Chicago School to the great social encyclicals
   of the popes.[36] It provides motivation for a
   certain mission or involvement and offers some
   basic insights into anthropology, particularly
   the values of freedom and solidarity.
   (-) The model is reductionist, and highly selective

in its use of Scripture, making almost exclusive use of those Scriptural passages that speak of Jesus the servant. Moreover, the model can encompass a deficient anthropology insofar as it develops a theory of the human person on the basis of fringe experiences. For example, the anthropology of the ethical liberator model may well proclaim the dignity of the homosexual but it is lacking in an adequate understanding of human sexuality, heterosexuality, marriage and family — surely significant elements of a comprehensive anthropology.

4. *The Human Face of God.*
   (+) This model has a strong foundation in Scripture as well as some basis in Christian tradition. It is conducive to belief in a way that is meaningful to persons who live in the twentieth century.[37] The model is theologically fruitful, providing as it does a basis and integrating factor for ecclesiology and sacramentology. To its "functional" Christology corresponds an "economical" theology.[38] Moreover it is conducive to the elaboration of a good Christian anthropology.
   (-) The apparent weakness of the model lies in its being prone to pietism and its not being particularly conducive to the building up of Christian community.

5. *The Man for Others.*
   (+) This model is grounded in the Scriptures, but the model does not appear frequently in the history of theology. An asset is that "it encourages people to believe precisely because it impels the faithful to fulfill their Christian mission."[39] Its strong anthropological underpinning also contributes to the utility of the model.
   (-) The theological utility of the model is limited insofar as it does not provide a sufficiently broad base.

6. *The Personal Savior.*
   (+) This model has a good foundation in Scripture and provides motivation for a Scripturally-grounded faith.
   (-) The theological fruitfulness of the model is extremely limited. It is, moreover, susceptible to heterodox deviation as the long history of "Enthusiasm"[40] shows.

160

(±) From the standpoint of anthropology, this model
is of mixed utility. It provides for a positive
self-understanding of those who have faith in
Jesus as their personal savior, but encourages a
negative judgement upon those who do not share
this faith. At root is an individualism which
neglects the social aspects of human personhood.

Each of the six models incorporates a very
important insight, but this insight is susceptible of
becoming a deviation if it is absolutized. The
incarnational model has served as the traditional
paradigm of Christology, but in O'Grady's estimation as
a viable vehicle for the expression of Christology in
the modern world it is the weakest of the models.[41]
O'Grady himself opts for "Jesus, the human face of God"
as the model that offers the greatest possibilities.[42]
It is therefore a viable paradigm of Christology for our
times.

Indeed, the weakness of the Human Face of God
model, cited in the foregoing evaluation, is not
intrinsic to the model itself and may be avoided if the
model is accepted in its fullest sense. When one takes
the human Jesus seriously, one notes that Jesus was
bound to others by ties of friendship (Martha and Mary,
for example), leadership (Peter and John, for example)
and family (Jn 2:1-12). Imitation of the human Jesus
can thus provide a base for the communitarian dimension
of human and Christian existence. A notion of mission
can arise from the awareness that just as Jesus was the
human face of God for others in his times, so today's
Christians[43] must be the face of God in our times. An
adequate view of the Resurrection recognizes that the
New Testament's resurrection narratives often focus on
commission and the gathering of the church.[44] These
notions of multi-dimensional ties, of mission, and
assembly are important elements for an adequate
understanding of what the Christian community is called
to be.

When, furthermore, reflections of a philosophical-
anthropological nature are brought to bear upon the
human Jesus it becomes clear that both individuality and
sociality are components of Jesus' humanity just as they
are components of the humanity of every person. This
type of philosophical reflection is not, however,
generally found in the writings of those who have opted
for the human face of God model. Indeed one striking
feature of the attractiveness of the model is that it
can be used without the necessity of extensive

161

philosophical reflection.  Whereas the incarnational model of Christology requires the use of language such as "hypostatic union" and evokes the notion of "transsubstantiation" in reference to the Eucharist, the human face of God model and the theological elaboration developed around it forego technical philosophical discussion (including analysis, distinctions, and technical terminology).

Of the three models of Christology "from below", the Ethical Liberator model, the Human Face of God model, and the Man for Others model, the Human Face of God model is the most adequate because it is the most comprehensive.  It can be taken as the paradigm of a Christology "from below".  In contrast, the incarnational model of Christology is the paradigm of a Christology "from above".  There can be little doubt that a Christology "from below" is that with which most contemporary Christians find themselves congenial.  Consequently, the Human Face of God model would appear to be the model of Christology most indicated for pastoral use today.

This practical judgement can and ought to be put into a very broad historical context.  In the earliest centuries of Christianity, it was reality from above which provided the warrants for human existence.  At the dawn of the Christian era myths were widely used to interpret and validate human experience.  The history of the New Testament, especially to the extent that it incorporated mythical language and appropriated Gnostic hymns, interpreted and validated the experience of Jesus of Nazareth in mythical terms.  Subsequently philosophy (Platonic, neo-Platonic, Aristotelian) was used to validate and interpret the Christian faith.  From the time of the Fathers until the development of the neo-Thomism the search for "the real" provided the key to the interpretation of the Christian experience and its Christology.  Reflections on essence and causality were of the greatest importance in the philosophical, as well as in the earlier (and admittedly quite different) mythological, understanding of human existence.  Nowadays, however, the search for meaning focuses on meaningfulness, value and utility.  Relatedness, rather than cause or essence, is seen as the key to understanding all that is.  The physical and behavioral sciences illustrate very well this contemporary human quest for understanding.  It is within the context of this shift from an "essentialist" to an "existentialist" understanding of existence — a very broad paradigmatic shift[45] — that we must place the shift from the incarnational model to the Human Face of God model as the practicable model of Christology.


## The Church

At this juncture in our search for models of theological reflection it must be noted that different ecclesiologies correspond to these different Christologies.[46] O'Grady explained that "an example from the history of theology should help to clarify... In medieval times the model of Jesus as the ultimate ruler of all gave birth to a sense of judgment and control that produced an authoritarian Church in the late Middle Ages. If Jesus controlled all people and if the Church shared in this power, then the Church had an obligation to rule over everyone and consequently the Church could forbid anyone to think differently from the official teaching. Church leaders also saw themselves empowered to dethrone kings and force infidels to submit to baptism. The model was taken not from the role of Jesus in the gospels, but from the experience of secular, civil authority. Turning Jesus into a secular potentate and then using that model to control the society from which it arose demonstrates just how questionable that particular model was from the outset."[47]

Since Christology is the foundation of ecclesiology, we can attempt to trace the models of ecclesiology which cohere with the different models of Christology. There will not be perfect congruence between the six models which result from this reflection and the five models of the church offered by Dulles in the analysis surveyed in the previous chapter. The discrepancy partially arises because O'Grady has discerned six models of Christology whereas Dulles has identified only five models of ecclesiology. More fundamentally, however, the discrepancy exists because we are dealing with "models", not clearly identifiable individual realities which can be adequately separated from other realities.

The incarnational model of Christology[48] offers a crystal clear ecclesiological model. Since it focuses on, "a God-man directing things to his purpose," "an ecclesiology based on this model tends to share in the omniscience, giving clear, objective principles of moral conduct. Jesus spoke authoritatively to his church for all times and circumstances since he spoke from the

163

eternity of God. Jesus foresaw his Church with its sacramental system and positions of authority and affirmed the entire process based upon his decision and knowledge as the Second Person of the Blessed Trinity. The Church's theology followed suit."[49]

A church whose practical Christology coheres with the incarnational model is one which teaches with confident authority; it is one with clearly defined structures. The authority of its teaching comes from the "revelation" upon which it is grounded. Theology subsequently becomes largely an effort to interpret and support official pronouncements of the teaching authority, for example, the teachings of the Magisterium among Roman Catholics or the words of Scripture among evangelicals. A heavily metaphysical construct will pervade both systematic theology and Christian ethics. In parallel fashion, the structures of the church are clearly defined because they represent the will of the omniscient law-giver, the divine person himself. Consequently it appears that the model of ecclesiology which coheres with the incarnational model of Christology is the institutional church. It is a church such as it existed in Roman Catholicism prior to the Second Vatican Council (and since).

The mythological model of Christology is one which makes the church almost redundant. Christology itself suffers the loss of its specificity, and maybe its very identity, when the mythological model is embraced. *A fortiori* the church loses the *raison d'être* of its specific existence, and perhaps the very reason for its existence itself. Much about the church is myth, and needs to be demythologized; the rites of the church are dramatic myths of low mimetic nature. In short, the church in the traditional sense is rendered virtually superflous by the mythological model of Christology.

The ethical liberator model of Christology has tremendous implications for ecclesiology, particularly in regard to church practice. The church which espouses Jesus as the Liberator will be a church which is highly committed to social justice. It will be a church that is involved with the political process. It is a church which identifies with the poor and the oppressed. This church has had its martyrs, such as Archbishop Romero of San Salvador.[50] The church, thus committed, is a church which has a keen sense of mission, even if the mission is somewhat narrowly conceived. It is a church characterized by elements frequently subsumed under the kerygmatic and servant models of ecclesiology.

164

In regards to the correlation between a Human Face of God Christology and ecclesiology O'Grady has written: "The human face of God affects Christian anthropology as well as questions related to morality and the meaning of the Church. Ecclesiology in particular is affected, since there is a parallel in the understanding of Jesus as the human face of God and the Church as the sacrament of Jesus in the world today. This involves every aspect of the Church, not just its hierarchy and sacraments. Where the Church is, Jesus is. The praying Church, the consoling Church, the reconciler, the serving Church, fulfills its destiny as the presence of Jesus in the world today. The very human Church reflects the divine Jesus."[51]

An ecclesiology related to the human face of God Christology clearly corresponds to Dulles' "church as sacrament" model of ecclesiology. It is a church which sees itself as a community of faith in which the proclamation of the resurrection of Jesus of Nazareth is central to its existence.[52] In this sense the church is an Easter community. Since the resurrection is strongly attested by the Scriptures of the New Testament, the Bible, and especially the New Testament, has an important place in the piety and theologizing of a church of this type.

The man for others model of Christology implies a church which cannot be removed from the market place nor remain indifferent to the suffering of peoples. It "identifies the Church as a group within which the man for others continues his work of reconciling and restoring. The corollary of the view of Jesus as the man for others accomplishing the reconciliation and restoration is a Church continuing this mission through the activity of its members."[53] This is a church which identifies with those who are crying out in need. Like the crucified Jesus[54] himself, this church is willing to bear pain and suffering as it reaches out to those in need. This is the servant church.

Finally, the model of Jesus, personal savior, also has ecclesiological implications. The embrace of Jesus as personal savior evokes evangelical Christians, with their characteristic life-style. The model suggests that the bond of Christian unity is a personal faith in Jesus the savior. The church is seen as the broad community of faith, as a loose association of like-minded, believing Christians. Consequently denominational ties are of lesser significance. A sort of panecumenism results. Indeed the charismatic renewal

165

within the contemporary Roman Catholicism offers a
typical practical experience of this type of
ecclesiology. The service of the Word and the prayer
group are all important. The Eucharist loses its place
as the central element of the Christian community.[55]
Charismatic groups are frequently characterized by a
very "open-minded" ecumenism.[56] One could say that the
model of church which corresponds to that of Jesus as
personal savior is the church as community, provided
that one allows for an understanding of community
different from that commonly held by the mainline
churches. Nonetheless a still more fundamental insight
into the nature of charismatic communities can be had
when these are seen as representative of the kerygmatic
model of church.

*A Brief Reflection*

In terms of the ITT, the foregoing reflection on
the relationship between Christology and ecclesiology
can be schematized in the following fashion:

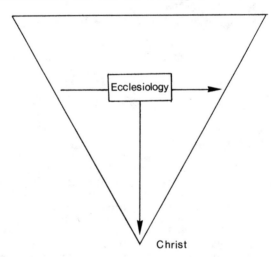

What the church specifically signifies intimates a
particular Christology. The church is a community of
believers who have faith in Christ. The way a faith
community lives is a sign of its understanding of the
Christ. An operative ecclesiology carried over into
practice is a clear sign of a Christological belief.

What this suggests in terms of a reflection on ministry is that there is a relationship between one's ministry and one's functional (or operative) Christology. One's ministry implies one's Christology. This results from the fact that one's ministry is a sign of one's operative ecclesiology together with the additional fact that one's practical ecclesiology is a sign of one's operative Christology. According to the categories of linguistic analysis, one should therefore consider that one's ecclesiology and one's Christology belong to the same "sign system". Together they constitute a large measure of the realities implied along the syntactic axis when one's ministry is analyzed by means of the ITT:

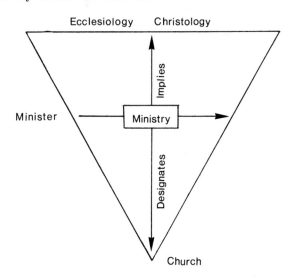

One's ministry reflects one's Christological option. Implicit in one's ministry is one's practical faith in Jesus (one's operative Christology). That is, wherever the Christian is involved in ministerial activity he/she is signifying a particular modality of faith in Christ.

At this point it becomes vitally important to recall that in the hierarchy of truths,[57] it is Christology which should be determinative of one's ecclesiology (and consequently of one's ministerial activity). Virtually all ecclesiological reflection includes the notion that the church is dependent on the reality of Jesus Christ. The institutional model of

167

church suggests, for example, that the church is what it
is because it was "founded by Jesus Christ". The
sacramental model of the church suggests that the church
is what it is since Jesus was who he was and since he is
still present in the church through the Resurrection-
gift of the Spirit. In sum, it is Christology which
provides the principal elements for a theological
critique of one's ecclesiology, as well as of that
ministry which signifies one's ecclesiological option.

1.  John F. O'Grady, *Models of Jesus* (Garden City: Doubleday, 1981).

2.  According to O'Grady, John McIntyre was the first theologian to develop a models approach to Christology. See John McIntyre, *The Shape of Christology* (London: SCM, 1966); cf. J. F. O'Grady, *op. cit.*, p. 35, n. 29.

3.  D. S. 148.

4.  See Philipp Kaiser, *Das Wissen Jesu Christi in der lateinischen, westlichen, Theologie. Eichstätter Studien*, 14 (Regensburg: Pustet, 1981).

5.  J. F. O'Grady, *op. cit.*, p. 4.

6.  Jacques Guillet began his book on the consciousness of Jesus in this fashion: "What relation is there between Jesus' consciousness and the faith of his disciples? The answer is apparently simple and free of all ambiguity: the faith of his disciples rests on the consciousness of Jesus. He knew he was the Son of God, he revealed it to his disciples and proved it by rising from the dead." J. Guillet, *The Consciousness of Jesus* (New York: Newman, 1972), p. 3,

7.  Raymond Brown has suggested that only three texts in the New Testament explicitly calls Jesus "God". They are Heb 1:8-9; John 1:1; and John 20:28. See R. E. Brown, *Jesus, God and Man. Modern Philosophical Reflections* (Milwaukee: Bruce, 1967).

8.  J. F. O'Grady, *op. cit.*, p. 54.

9.  See D. F. Strauss, *The Life of Jesus Critically Examined* (Philadelphia: Fortress, 1973).

10. John A. T. Robinson, *Honest to God* (London: SCM, 1963). See further John A. T. Robinson-David L. Evans, *The Honest to God Debate. Some Reaction to the Book Honest to God* (London: SCM, 1963).

11. John Heck, ed., *The Myth of God Incarnate* (London: SCM, 1977). See further Michael Goulder, ed., *Incarnation and Myth. The Debate Continued* (London: SCM, 1979).

12. See Rudolf Bultmann, *Kerygma and Myth* (New York: Harper and Row, 1961); *Jesus Christ and Mythology*

(New York: Scribners, 1958).

13. See James P. Mackey, *Jesus, the Man and the Myth. A Contemporary Christology* (London: SCM, 1979).

14. J. Sobrino, *Christology at the Crossroads* (Maryknoll: Orbis, 1978); L. Boff, *Jesus Christ Liberator* (Maryknoll: Orbis, 1978).

15. See Brian Mullady, "An Analysis of Christology in Liberation Theology," *Angelicum* 58 (1981) 438-459, esp. pp. 457-459 where Mullady offers a summation of his critique: "First, the consequences of political-liberation theology for the doctrine of Christ as the Son of God are seriously superficial. This is because they are based on a superficial idea of man.... Second, this superficial idea of man leads to a very superficial idea of social unity. Freedom is simply allowing the other to act.... Third, the notion of theology as a sort of State Department of morals to bless the proper civil powers is also very superficial. Indeed, when the Church becomes wedded to any social order as such, all those who are not a part of this particular order are not only expendable, but enemies of the Church and State.... Fourth, the greatest problem of all is the notion of Christ and his body. In positing Christ simply as the great social reactor, all the real content of Christ as he who reveals eternity and the supernatural order to us is compromised... " From this last emphasis it is clear the Mullady's criticism proceeds from the incarnational model of Christology. (It must also be noted that Mullady was reacting more to the Christologies of J. B. Metz and G. Gutierrez than to the explicitly Christological studies of Sobrino and Boff.)

16. See Richard P. McBrien, *art. cit.*, p. 145.

17. See Mark Schoof, "Dutch Catholic Theology: A New Approach to Christology," *Cross Currents* 22 (1973) 415-427.

18. Cf. Piet Schoonenberg, *The Christ* (New York: Herder and Herder, 1971); Stephen Pujdak, "Schoonenberg's Christology in Context," *Louvain Studies* 6 (1976-1977) 338-353.

19. See Ansfried Hulsbosch, "Jezus Christus, gekend als mens, beleden als Zoon Gods," *Tijdschrift voor*

*Theologie* 6 (1966) 250-273.

20. See E. Schillebeeckx, *Jesus. An Experiment in Christology* (New York: Seabury, 1979). *Christ. The Experience of Jesus as Lord* (New York: Seabury, 1980). Even before the publication of these first two volumes in Schillebeeckx' Christological trilogy, some insights into Schillebeeckx' Christology could be gleaned from reading his *Christ, The Sacrament of the Encounter with God* (London: Sheed and Ward, 1963). See Robert Brown, *The Myth of God Incarnate: A Contemporary Re-appraisal of the Doctrine of the Incarnation.* Unpublished licentiate thesis, Louvain, 1979, pp. 104-111.

21. Joseph Ratzinger, presently prefect of the Congregation for the Faith, was the third member of the triumvirate.

22. That is, rather than within a context of Trinitarian theology, the theological context of the incarnational model of Christology.

23. Cf. Piet Schoonenberg, "Process or History in God," *Louvain Studies* 4 (1972-1973) 303-319.

24. See Joachim Jeremias, *The Prayers of Jesus. Studies in Biblical Theology*, 2nd. series, 6 (London: SCM, 1967), pp. 11-65.

25. J. F. O'Grady, *op. cit.*, p. 101.

26. *Idem.*, p. 104.

27. The advantages of overcoming this dichotomy are to be evaluated within the context of the decade-long debate on the relationship between the natural and the supernatural.

28. C. W. Morris, *art. cit.*, see above, p. 148, n. 5.

29. Pantheism must be distinguished from panentheism, as elaborated by Hartshorne. See Charles B. Hartshorne, "Can we understand God," *Louvain Studies* 7 (1978-1979) 75-84; Jan Van der Veken, "A Conversation Between Charles Hartshorne and Jan Van der Veken," *Louvain Studies* 8 (1980-1981) 129-142.

30. Especially *Letters and Papers from Prison* (rev.

ed.: New York: Macmillan, 1967) and, *The Cost of Discipleship* (New York: Macmillan, 1967).

31. J. A. T. Robinson, *Honest to God* (Philadelphia: Westminster, 1963).

32. For example, in 1 Thess 1:10.

33. See "Yves Congar on the Holy Spirit," *Louvain Studies* 6 (1976-1977) 179-181, p. 180.

34. See "Evaluating the Models," Chapter IX of *Models of Jesus*, pp. 169-179.

35. See further Tom F. Driver, *Christ in a Changing World. Toward an Ethical Christology* (London: SCM, 1981).

36. From Leo XIII's *Rerum Novarum* to John Paul II's *Laborem Exercens*.

37. See E. Schillebeeckx who has written, "... in a like regard for faith and human reason I want to look for what a Christological belief in Jesus of Nazareth can intelligibly signify for people today." E. Schillebeeckx, *Jesus*, p. 33.

38. See M. R. E. Masterson, "Economy, Divine," *New Catholic Encyclopedia* 5 (New York: McGraw-Hill, 1967), p. 86.

39. J. F. O'Grady, *op. cit.*, p. 174.

40. See Ronald Knox, *Enthusiasm* (New York: Oxford University Press, 1949).

41. See J. F. O'Grady, *op. cit.*, p. 177.

42. *Ibid.*

43. See Rom 6:5, literally, "united with him in similarity" (εἰ γὰρ σύμφυτοι γεγόναμεν τῷ ὁμοιώματι).

44. See especially Matt 28:16-20, cf. Mark 16:16. In O'Grady's terms, "the resurrection and the assembling are two facets of one event." See J. F. O'Grady, *op. cit.*, p. 107.

45. See Jerome T. Walsh, "Being Theologians in a Paradigm Shift," *Louvain Studies* 9 (1982-1983)

116-121.

46. Apropos the correlation, see, for example, J. Peter Schineller, "Christ and Church: A Spectrum of Views," *Theological Studies* 37 (1976) 545-566.

47. J. F. O'Grady, *op. cit.*, p. 31.

48. *Idem.*, pp. 52-53.

49. *Idem.*, p. 53.

50. See "Archbishop Oscar Romero," *Louvain Studies* 8 (1980-1981) pp. 194-195.

51. J. F. O'Grady, *op. cit.*, p. 113.

52. The centrality of the resurrection as a dimension of ecclesial self-understanding is clearly brought out by Schillebeeckx in *Christ, the Sacrament of the Encounter with God.*

53. See J. F. O'Grady, *op. cit.*, p. 121.

54. The centrality of the crucifixion as a primary religious symbol of the "Man for Others" Christology points to the Lutheran context out of which this approach to Christology arose.

55. *Econtra*, Vatican Council II: "... the Eucharistic Sacrifice, which is the fount and apex of the whole Christian life... " (*Lumen Gentium*, 11 in *Documents*, p. 28); "... the liturgy is the summit towards which the activity of the Church is directed; at the same time it is the fountain from which all her power flows. ... From the liturgy, therefore, and especially from the Eucharist... " (*Sacrosanctum Concilium*, 10 in *Documents*, p. 142).

56. Nonetheless there is generally a tightly-knit disciplinary/organizational structure within the charismatic churches. See, for example, Ralph Philip Martin, *The Family and the Fellowship. New Testament Images of the Church* (Exeter: Pater Noster, 1979).

57. See *Unitatis Redintegratio*, 11: "when comparing doctrines, they should remember that in Catholic teaching there exists an order or 'hierarchy' of truths, since they vary in their relationship to the foundation of the Christian faith" (*Documents*,

354).

Chapter Eleven


The Scriptural Model


*A Critique through the Medium of the Word*

If one's Christological reflection provides the
raw material for a critique of one's ecclesiology and
consequent ministerial practice, one might ask how one
might go about making a choice of the different models
of Christology. How does one judge the different
Christological options which are available? A first
criterion[1] would seem to be the Scriptures, especially
the Scriptures of the New Testament. "The Scripture",
John Leith has written, "has remained as a check on
tradition and as a paradigm of Christian experience.
The historical fact is that Christian theology without
Scripture is practically unthinkable."[2]

Indeed the Scriptures are the *norma non normata*
(the un-normed norm) of the theological endeavor. If
the Scriptures are to function within the life of the
church in this capacity, it would seem that the
Scriptures are both an essential source for the doing of
theology and that they exercise a critical function in
evaluating theology. Indeed, the Scriptures would seem
to have a function that is at once constitutive,
critical, indicative, provocative, and validating with
regards to theology.[3]

It is in the critical function of the Scriptures
that we must be most interested at the present time
since our presentation of five interlocking models of
theological reflection has proceeded from the level of
understanding to the level of judging ministerial
experience.[4] In fact the Scriptures have a double role
in the evaluation of ministerial experience. On the one
hand, they exercise a critical function with respect to
that in terms of which ministerial experience is an
expression. The Scriptures should serve as a critique
of the ecclesial and Christological models in terms of
which ministerial experience is to be understood and
judged. On the other hand, the Scriptures can and ought
to be used in a more immediate fashion as a medium of
reflection, interpretation, and evaluation of the
ministerial experience itself.

175

When one arrives at this type of awareness and wishes to proceed further, to a consideration of the precise way in which the Scriptures can serve a critical function in the process of theological reflection, understood both broadly and concretely, one has entered into an area which is the object of much reflection within the church at the present time.[5] In the Protestant tradition, the issue has been phrased in terms of the authority of the Scriptures. If the Scriptures are to be interpreted from the standpoint of historical criticism, just what is their authority?[6] In Roman Catholicism, the issue takes the form of an attempt to make Scriptures "the soul of theology" (*anima sacrae theologiae*).[7] How, in fact, does one employ the Scriptures in the development and exposition of systematic theology?

Two extremes must be avoided. On the one hand, the scriptural component of theological reflection must avoid a naive fundamentalism. A fundamentalist approach to the Scriptures represents a naive attempt to return to a past which can no longer be recuperated. We should not think that the Scriptures provide a ready-made response to the situations confronting the church today. On the other hand, the use of Scriptures in theological reflection must avoid a proof-text type of citation. It is not a matter of finding an isolated verse of Scripture which seemingly provides a warrant for one's ecclesiology and/or ministry. One can make the Scriptures support almost anything whatsoever, since there is always at least one verse to support a given position or an action. At best the proof-text approach represents an "icing on the cake" technique. Because the Scriptures are the *norma non normata* and the soul of theology, we should be looking for a use of the Scriptures which will enable them to permeate our theological reflection.

This use of the Scriptures should be one in which the Scriptures are critically interpreted. They are not a narrative account of a timeless myth, they are rather a concrete and historically-conditioned faith witness. If the Scriptures, critically interpreted, are to be used in theological reflection, several difficulties must be overcome,[8] for example, the attempt to solve modern critical problems on the basis of dogmatic statements phrased in a pre-critical era. One should not appeal too quickly to the principle that a specific practice or form of ministry was instituted by Christ and that therefore it is timelessly normative. One must also be wary of the forced interpretation of the silence

of the New Testament in the light of later dogmatic
interests. Often silence is an indication that a later
doctrinal position was not even an issue in New
Testament times. We must also be sensitive to a given
tradition's tendency to neglect or underplay texts that
do not accord with later dogmatic positions.

### A Legitimate and Necessary Task

Within this perspective, it can be affirmed that
it is both legitimate and necessary for us to bring
Scriptures to bear interpretatively and critically upon
our ecclesial (or ministerial) experience. The
legitimacy of this use of Scriptures is based upon the
fact that the church has always used the Scriptures in
this fashion.[9] From the time of the first formulations
of the faith,[10] and throughout the history of the church,
the Scriptures have been normatively used as a means for
interpreting the Christian experience.

The written gospels bear witness to the fact that
the Gospel tradition itself was used to interpret the
later experience of the church. A classic example is
the parable of the Sower.[11] The parable itself (Mark
4:3-9) lies on the firm ground of the Jesus tradition.
The interpretation of the parable (Mark 4:13-20)[12]
brings the parable to bear upon the situation of the
church in later times. Were one to delete the agrarian
imagery from the explanation, one would be left with
vocabulary typical of the way the church described the
proclamation of the word and its reception.[13] Thus the
church used the parable of the sower as a vehicle of
reflection on the fact that not everyone received the
gospel which it proclaimed.

In a similar sort of way, Matthew used the
traditional story of the Stilling of the Storm[14] as a
means of reflecting on the nature of discipleship. As a
matter of fact recent redaction critical studies of the
Gospels have tended to single out the editorial
emendations of later authors upon the earlier Gospel
tradition. To some extent these emendations can be
viewed as an accommodation    (actualization) of the
traditional material; from another point of view, they
can be seen as an attempt to interpret the experience of
the later church in the light of an earlier tradition.

Even more radically, it should be noted that the
church of New Testament times frequently interpreted its

own experience by means of the Old Testament Scriptures (the Bible). Thus the apostle Paul evaluated his experience in the light of the model of the Servant of Yahweh.[15] Similarly, the Johannine community looked at the Eucharist in the light of the gift of Manna to Israel at the time of the Exodus.[16]

The interpretation of ecclesial existence in the light of the Scriptural tradition and by means of the language of that tradition, so typical of the church in its formative years, has remained characteristic of the church throughout its history. During the Patristic and early medieval periods, theology was considered to be the exposition of the *sacra pagina*. It was the meaning of the Scriptures which determined the church's reflective thought during those times. More recently, the biblical renewal[17] was one of the factors in the church of the mid-twentieth century which gave occasion to the Second Vatican Council. When the Council was convened and the fathers began their examination of the church, they chose to do so formally by means of the Scriptures. Thus there is a kerygmatic air to the reflection on the Church found in the Dogmatic Constitution, *Lumen Gentium*,[18] one of the foundational documents[19] of the council. Moreover, this document chose to describe the church, in the first instance, by means of biblical categories, notably the image of the People of God.[20]

It is not only legitimate for the reflective minister of the church to use the Scriptures interpretatively and critically in reflecting on the church and its ministry, it is also necessary for the minister to do so. Radically, this is due to the fact that the Scriptures are a constitutive element of the Church. The Eucharistic liturgy serves as a sign that the Scriptures are a constitutive element of the church. The Eucharistic celebration is a sort of cameo or miniature of the church. As *the* sacrament of the church, it is a sign of what the church is. The liturgy of the word (that is the proclamation and exposition of the Scriptures) is, however, an integral part of the eucharistic liturgy.[21] In this fashion the church itself symbolizes that the Scriptures belong to its very essence.

When groups of radical Christians have replaced the reading of passages from the canonical Scriptures in the liturgy with readings from modern (and even secular) authors, ecclesiastical authorities have been quick and unanimous in their reaction. They have indicated that readings from modern authors may be incorporated into the liturgy (at various appropriate places) but that they may never replace the readings of the Scriptures. In like vein, it is to be noted that church authorities have repeatedly appealed to those who preside at the eucharistic liturgy to respect the biennial and triennial cycles of Scriptural readings[22] stipulated by the liturgical norms of the church. Part of the motivation for this type of intervention is surely disciplinary. Yet part of it has to do with the nature of the relationship between the Scriptures and the church. The church is not free to pick and choose from among the Scriptures; rather it is to be addressed by the Scriptures which then form a heuristic "angle of vision" from which the church can understand its own experience.

Another striking indication of the fact that the Scriptures are a constitutive element of the church is the fact that the second of the two dogmatic constitutions issued by the Second Vatican Council was *Dei Verbum*. As *Lumen Gentium*, so *Dei Verbum* is a foundational document.[23] It speaks of the church's essential awareness. The topic of this important document is Divine Revelation, particularly as this is attested by the Scriptures.

## The Evolving Church

A use of the Scriptures in theological reflection is one which will be attentive to the Scriptures in their coming into being. It will take into account the fact of development in the life of the church as well as the fact of the development of the church's self-understanding to which the Scriptures themselves give witness. This development took place under the guidance of the Holy Spirit. Acceptance of the Scriptures as a hermeneutical tool for understanding and judging the experience of the church today requires that the minister take this development seriously. This development is a major indication that a Scriptural reflection on the church and its ministry cannot proceed from a fundamentalist, static, once-for-all interpretation of the text. The Scriptures attest that there is development. There will continue to be development in the church's life and understanding because of the presence within it of that same Spirit which inspired the Scriptures.

Development can be seen in the Old Testament as well as in the New Testament. It is well known that the

Decalogue appears in two major versions in the Old
Testament: Exod 20:1-17, and Deut 5:6-21, and that the
Exodus version represents, by and large, the more
ancient tradition.[24] According to the Revised Standard
Version, the "eighth" precept of the Decalogue is:
"Neither shall you bear false witness against your
neighbor." From the similar reading of the English-
language version in Deut 5:20 and Exod 20:10, one would
suppose that there was a same Hebrew Text which was
translated. In fact the verb *šaw* is found in Exod 20
whereas the verb *šeger* is used in Deut 5:20. The New
American Bible attempted to capture the significance of
the different readings of the Hebrew text by rendering
the Exodus text as "You shall not bear false witness
against your neighbor," and the Deuteronomic text as
"You shall not bear dishonest witness... " There is, in
fact, a difference of nuance between *šaw* and *šeger*. The
primary connotation of *šaw* is "false", whereas the
primary connotation of *šeger* is "disloyal". Conceivably
it would be possible to "tell the truth" (half-truth,
circumlocutions, mental reservations) and not serve the
cause of justice. Thus the reading *šaw* was found to be
inadequate to the purpose of the commandment. The later
version was formulated so as to exclude all testimony
that did not serve the cause of justice.

A comparison of the two canonical versions of the
Parable of the Great Banquet[25] (from the Q tradition)
can serve as an indication of the manner in which the
church of the New Testament times was wary lest a
literalistic interpretation of the tradition run counter
to the Spirit's purposes within the church. Lest the
gratuitous offer of divine salvation be seen as an
indication that the quality of one's response to the
invitation be taken as of no consequence, Matthew has
appended to the traditional tale his little story of the
wedding garment (Matt 22:11-14). With this addendum,
Matthew has cautioned against a false security which
thinks that God's salvation is "in the bag".[26]

### An Angle of Vision

Theological reflection which is Scripturally
based, oriented, and inspired, is one in which the New
Testament itself provides an angle of vision.

To speak of the New Testament in this sense is to
speak of the New Testament in its entirety. The one who
uses the Scriptures in theological reflection must

180

accept the entire canon of the New Testament. It is the canon of the Scriptures which is the *norma non normata*, the norm of faith. This is the catholic principle in the use of the Scriptures. According to this principle, the use of a "canon within a canon" is not acceptable.[27]

While the catholic principle of New Testament interpretation precludes the acceptance of a "canon within the canon", honesty demands that oftentimes the principle has been operative more in the breach of it than in loyalty to it. While Protestants (especially within the Reform tradition) have tended to accept Paul but not Matthew; Catholics have — in the practical order — tended to accept Matthew but not Paul. In the elaboration of Mariology, Catholics easily accept Luke and John, but are not as open to what the Markan and Matthean narratives say about the mother of Jesus.[28] Catholics accept some elements of church order on the basis of the Pastorals (the three degrees of hierarchy, for example), but they are not generally as ready to accept other elements which are also indicated in this section of the New Testament (the deaconess of 1 Tim 2:11, for example).

Not only is it necessary for the one who is engaged in theological reflection to accept the New Testament in its entirety, it is also necessary that the one who reflects accepts the diversity and unity of the New Testament.[29] Any dogmatic reductionism is to be ruled out of order on the basis of the New Testament itself. Within the New Testament there are different Christologies. Matthew's Christology is different from that of Paul.[30] The "adoptionist" Christology of Acts 2:36 is different from the incarnational Christology of John 1:1-18. There are different ecclesiologies in the New Testament. The church order reflected by the Pastorals (and Matthew) is different from the charismatic ordering of the Corinthian and Thessalonian communities. There are somewhat different ethical norms in the New Testament. The radical version of Jesus' logion on divorce found in Mark and Luke differs from the accommodations found in Matthew and Paul. Indeed, we could point to differences at every turn when we compare the witness of the New Testament documents among themselves. Nonetheless there is a basic unity since these various faith witnesses belong to the single canon of the New Testament.

The one who seriously reflects on the unity and diversity of the various elements of the New Testament, soon realizes that a creative tension exists among these disparate elements. Moreover he or she will quickly discover that some of the diverse elements are relatively compatable whereas some others are difficult, if not impossible, to reconcile.[31] Thus Matthew focuses on Jesus' post-resurrectional presence to the church in his word, whereas John emphasizes the gift of the Spirit and the gift of mutual love[32] as the mode of Jesus' presence to his community after the return to the Father. There is no great difficulty in thinking of three different modes of Jesus' presence in the church: presence through his word, presence through his Spirit, and presence through a dynamic love. On the other hand, it is difficult to see how the biblical tradition of the virginal conception can be reconciled to an incarnational Christology.[33] That differences between the various components of the New Testament exposition are difficult to reconcile does not mean that they cannot be reconciled. Yet one must recognize that they oftentimes have not been reconciled within the New Testament itself, and that their common presence is a creative tension within the church.

In fact, when reflecting on the relationship between the Scriptures and ministerial experience, one should be aware that the relationship is essentially a dialogical one. One can proceed from a reflection on the Scriptures to a reflection on ministry; or one can reflect on ministry in the light of Scriptures. When one takes the former tack one will find that the use of the Scriptures frequently fulfills a function which I have elsewhere[34] described as being provocative and innovative. When one takes the latter tack, one will find that the use of Scriptures is occasionally critical, but oftentimes validating.


### Reflections on Ministerial Experience

*Example 1: Paul's Teaching on Charisms.*
It is generally acknowledged that the Pauline teaching on charisms was due to the religious genius of the apostle himself. That teaching is most comprehensively expressed in 1 Cor 12-14. When critically analyzed, these three chapters provide a paradigm for a reflection on ministry in the church today. Elements of a critique of charismatic phenomena within the church are provided in the opening verses.[35] A charismatic (whether we are dealing with an individual or a group seems to matter but little) can be judged to be authentic only when the charism is exercised within

the context of prayer, faith in the resurrection of
Jesus, and the acceptance of Jesus' Lordship over one's
life.

Beyond that the authentic charismatic can be
recognized by an exericse of the charism in accordance
with three by-words which encapsulate Paul's teaching on
charisms: "To each his own"... "With one another, for
one another"... "In obedience to the Lord"[36]... "To each
his own" rules out all forms of ecclesial egalitarianism
as well as all forms of church order which reduce
ministry to an oligarchic or monarchic form.  It
requires that the ministry of each member of the church
be recognized, for there is no baptized member of the
church who does not have a ministry (that is a charism).
"With one another, for one another" implies that there
is a vision of shared ministry to be held within the
church.  Ministry must be seen as a ministry on behalf
of others — a ministry of service rather than a ministry
which fulfills one's own needs or desires: a ministry of
service rather than a ministry of self-fulfillment.  All
ministry should lead to the upbuilding of the church as
the body of Christ, rather than to its fragmentation and
destruction.  "In obedience to the Lord" demands not
only that one be truly responsible before the Lord for
the way in which one fulfills one's own ministry, but
that one is also sensitive to the Lord who speaks
through other Christians who also possess the Spirit of
the Lord.  Were the ministers of the church to recognize
the authority of the Spirit of the Lord in others, it is
clear that many of the contemporary difficulties of the
church could be overcome.  A charismatic understanding
of the church is one which evokes mutual obedience.
Would this principle not be fruitful indeed in a church
presently characterized by tensions between pastors and
their flocks, the clergy and the laity, bishops and
priests, the magisterium and theologians?[37]

The recognition of the essentially charismatic
ordering of the church might well offer a paradigm for
the interpretation and judgment of certain problems in
practical ecclesiology.  The charisms offer a model of
reflection on unity and diversity.  Is it impossible
that such a model might provide a paradigm for a
possible mode of union between Rome and Canterbury?
Indeed, doesn't the presence of different charisms in
the church offer a perspective from which one might come
to grips with problems arising from the need to
inculturate the Gospel in various cultures?

*Example 2: Matthew's Version of the Parable of the Lost Sheep.*
It is well known that the parable of the lost sheep has come down to us in four versions.[38] Each of the versions gives evidence of editorial activity on the part of their respective authors. The Matthean version[39] has been so modified as to constitute a challenge for church leaders. While the disciples at large are exhorted not to despise the "little ones", the leaders of the church are challenged to seek out those who have gone astray. Indeed, "one might draw from the dogmatic statement of v. 14 the conclusion that the Father's will that no one of the little ones come to grief is realized insofar as priests go in search of the little ones who have gone astray, no matter the reason why they have strayed from the flock."[40]

In sum, Matthew's version of the parable of the lost sheep offers a reflection on ministry which is a challenge to a stay-at-home life-style. It should confront those who see their ministry as being almost exclusively directed to the committed members of a parish or church group. Oftentimes those who are entrusted with a ministry of leadership within the church see themselves as called to minister only to those who are active members of the church. Their ministry has often been characterized as a ministry to the saved. The Matthean version of the Parable of the Lost Sheep serves to confront that type of ministry. The Jesuanic logian of Mark 2:17[41] provides a similar confrontation, albeit expressed in a different language.

*Example 3: "All things to all men."*
"All things to all men" is a citation taken from 1 Cor 9:22 but it often serves as a slogan for those who adopt a ministerial life style which involves them in every conceivable type of ministerial activity. Sometimes this style of ministry is not sensitive to the specificity of one's own charism. Frequently it leads to a fragmented type of ministry which the minister finds burdensome. It is generally accompanied by a notable lack of (ministerial) priorities. Sometimes it leads to the neglect of the needed care of self, a failure to attend to one's own family and coministers, and even a failure to attend to some forms of ministry for which the "all things to all men" minister is responsible — all because the minister refuses, in faith, to think about the meaning and priorities of ministry. Finally, and all too often, this type of ministry can result in a lack of personal integrity or "burnout".[42]

Reflection on the biblical theme of time brings to mind the adage "make the most of your time".[43] It recalls that time is of God's creation. There is time for everything — including laughter, embracing, and losing.[44] A distinction is to be made between *chronos* time and *kairos* time. It is only *kairos* time which is truly critical, since *kairos* time in the New Testament is eschatological time. The Jesus of the New Testament is one who took leave of his disciples in order to go into the hills and pray.[45] The biblical understanding of time thus offers a critical grid[46] for reflection on ministerial hyperactivity.

*Example 4:    The Liturgical Ministry.*

Those who find that their conscious priorities are such that they put the liturgical ministry (celebration of Eucharist and sacraments, liturgical preaching, and so forth) at the top of their list as well as those who discover from an assessment of their use of time that liturgical celebration is an operative priority in their lives might well reflect on the mission theme in the New Testament.

The "I have come"[47] statements reflect the early church's understanding of Jesus' mission. The programmatic statements of Mark 1:15 and Luke 4:16-21 (30) point to Jesus' ministry as one of preaching and healing. The mission discourses of the Synoptic tradition[48] put the mission of the disciples in a similar frame of reference. Luke's vision of the activity of the early church such as it is portrayed in Acts and Paul's statements about the understanding of his own ministry[49] offer  some suggestion for a Christian vision of ministry. Even the Great Commission of Matt 28:16-20[50] indicates that there is a ministry of teaching which is to accompany the ministry of baptizing.

*A Brief Reflection*

Evidently the one who allows the Scriptures to address his or her ministerial experience is not going to find in the Scriptures of the New Testament ready-made answers for the problems inherent in one's practical ministry; nor will he or she find in the New Testament an adequate paradigm for ministry in the 1980's. Nonetheless one who takes the Scriptures seriously will find in them an angle of vision, indeed a normative mode of understanding the radical Christian

experience, which ought to "inform"[51] ministerial
experience today.

When the doctrine of inspiration of the Scriptures
is taken in its broadest sense — that is as involving
not only passive inspiration but active inspiration as
well[52] — it will be seen that the Spirit who spoke to
the churches in times past through the Scriptures is
still speaking to the church through the Scriptures.
For the minister of the gospel, an openness to the
Scriptures and a willingness to allow them to exercise a
critical function vis-á-vis the ministry is simply an
openness to the Spirit, and a form of obedience to the
Lord.

1. Both Dulles and O'Grady cite "a firm basis in Scripture" as the first of the criteria for evaluating, respectively, the ecclesiological and christological models. See A. Dulles, *op. cit.*, p. 180; J. F. O'Grady, *op. cit.*, p. 170.

2. John H. Leith, "The Bible and Theology," *Interpretation* 30 (1976) 227-241, p. 227.

3. See R. F. Collins, *Introduction to the New Testament* (New York: Doubleday, 1983) 291-298.

4. See Raymond E. Brown, *Biblical Reflections on Crises Facing the Church* (New York: Paulist, 1975). The topics on which Brown has reflected are catechetics, the ordination of women, the papacy, the role of Mary, Christology, and ecumenism.

5. See David H. Kelsey, *The Uses of Scripture in Recent Theology* (London: SCM, 1975).

6. "Since the Bible has lost what authority it at one time had in its own right, and its principle significance for faith and theology is now its indispensibility as the primary collection of reports of the acts of God, it is essential that it be dealt with as any other historical source and be subjected to careful criticism at every point" (Gordon D. Kaufman).

7. *Dei Verbum*, 24 in *Documents*, p. 127; *Optatam Totius*, 16 in *Documents*, p. 451.

8. See Raymond E. Brown, "Difficulties in Using the New Testament in American Catholic Discussions," *Louvain Studies* 6 (1976-1977) 144-158, esp. pp. 151-157, reprinted in *The Critical Meaning of the Bible* (New York: Paulist, 1981).

9. See Barnabas Lindars, *New Testament Apologetic: The Doctrinal Significance of the Old Testament Quotations* (London: SCM, 1961).

10. Cf. 1 Cor 15:3-5.

11. Mark 4:1-9; par. Matt 13:1-9; Luke 8:4-8. See Jan Lambrecht, *Once More Astonished. The Parables of Jesus* (New York: Crossroad, 1981) 85-109.

12. Par. Matt 13:18-23; Luke 8:11-15.

13. See Paul's reflections on the acceptance of God's

word in 1 Thess 1-2.

14. Matt 8:23 (par. Mark 4:36-41; Luke 8:22-24). See Gunther Bornkammer's "The Stilling of the Storm in Matthew," in Gunther Bornkamm, G. Barth, H. J. Heid, *Tradition and Interpretation in Matthew. New Testament Library* (London: SCM, 1963), pp. 52-57; R. F. Collins, *Introduction*, pp. 225-229.

15. See Jerome Murphy-O'Connor, *Paul on Preaching* (London: Sheed & Ward, 1964), pp. 108-113.

16. See John 6:25-40.

17. See R. F. Collins, "The Biblical Renewal. A revival and a movement," *American College Bulletin* 38 (1959) 20-23, 131-147.

18. See J. R. Donahue, "Scripture: A Roman Catholic Perspective," *Review and Expositor* 79 (1982) 231-244.

19. Among the sixteen conciliar documents were two dogmatic constitutions, one constitution, one pastoral constitution, nine decrees, and three declarations. *Lumen Gentium* and *Dei Verbum* have the status of dogmatic constitutions. As such, they are analogous to the constitutions of modern political states. They reflect the essential and normative self-understanding of the church at the time of the council.

20. See *Lumen Gentium*, 9-17 in *Documents*, pp. 24-37. Other biblical images are adduced at the end of the chapter. See further the concluding words of *Lumen Gentium*, par. 69 in *Documents*, p. 96.

21. See *Sacrosanctum Concilium*, 56 in *Documents*, pp. 156-157; also par. 52 in *Documents*, p. 155.

22. See *Sacrosanctum Concilium*, 51 in *Documents*, p. 155.

23. "Important as the Constitution on the Church is generally agreed to be, it is equaled in stature by the Constitution on Divine Revelation; the two are the most fundamental documents produced by the Second Vatican Council. To the casual reader, the latter may not appear to be either novel or dramatic, but to the theologian it is of basic importance. Other constitutions and decrees will have more practical effects for people within the Church (e.g., the

Constitution on the Liturgy), or for those still
separated from her (e.g., the Decree on Ecumenism),
but all the documents depend on the faith in God's
word to men, which the Council has spelled out in
this Constitution." R. A. F. MacKenzie, in
*Documents*, p. 107.

24. See R. F. Collins, "The Ten Commandments in Current
Perspective," *The American Ecclesiastical Review*
161 (1969) 169-182.

25. Matt 22:1-14; Luke 14:15-24.

26. Eduard Schweizer, *The Good News According to
Matthew* (Atlanta: John Knox, 1975), p. 421.

27. In contrast, within the Reform tradition there has
been a two centuries' long discussion of the "canon
within the canon". See Inge Lönning, *"Kanon im
Kanon". Zum dogmatischen Grundlagenproblem des
neutestamentlichen Kanons. Forschungen zur
Geschichte und Lehre des Protestantismus* 63 (Oslo:
Universitets Forlaget, 1972).

28. See Raymond E. Brown, "Difficulties in Using the
New Testament," pp. 156-157.

29. See James D. G. Dunn, *The Unity and Diversity in
the New Testament. An Inquiry into the Character
of Earliest Christianity* (London: SCM, 1977).

30. Ivan Havener has also made the point that there
were different Christologies in the church before
Paul and that Paul integrated elements of these
different Christologies into 1 Thessalonians
without attempting to harmonize them. See I.
Havener, "The Pre-Pauline Christological Credal
Formulae of 1 Thessalonians," in *Society of
Biblical Literature 1981 Seminar Papers* (Chico:
Scholars Press, 1981) 105-128, p. 121.

31. See Ernst Käsemann, "The Canon of the New Testament
and the Unity of the Church," in *Essays on New
Testament Themes. Studies in Biblical Theology*
41 (London: SCM, 1960) 95-107, pp. 100-103.
Raymond E. Brown, *The Virginal Conception & Bodily
Resurrection of Jesus* (London: Geoffrey Chapman,
1973), pp. 42-47; *The Birth of the Messiah* (Garden
City: Doubleday, 1977), pp. 140-143.

32. See R. F. Collins, "'A New Commandment I Give to

You, that You Love One Another... ' (Jn 13:34)," *Laval théologique et philosophique* 35 (1979) 235-261, pp. 248-249.

33. See Wolfhart Pannenberg, *Jesus - God and Man* (Philadelphia: Westminster, 1968), p. 143; R. E. Brown, *The Virginal Conception*, p. 43.

34. See above, n. 3.

35. 1 Cor 12:1-2.

36. See Ernst Käsemann, "Ministry and Community in the New Testament," in *Essays on New Testament Themes*, 63-94, pp. 76-78.

37. See Yves Congar, "Bref histoire des formes du 'Magistère' et ses relations avec les docteurs," *Revue des sciences philosophiques et théologiques* 60 (1976) 99-112; Avery Dulles, *The Resilient Church. The Necessity and Limits of Adaptation* (Dublin: Gill and Macmillan, 1978), pp. 103-105.

38. Matt 18:10-14; Luke 15:1-7; Gospel of Thomas, 117; Gospel of Truth.

39. See R. F. Collins, "Parables for Priests: The Lost Sheep," *Emmanuel* 82 (1976) 578-584.

40. *Ibid.*, p. 583.

41. "Those who are well have no need of a physician, but those who are sick; I came not to call the righteous, but sinners." par. Matt 9:13; Luke 5:32.

42. See above, pp. 93, 98.

43. Eph 5:16.

44. Qoh 3:1-9.

45. Mark 6:46; par. Matt 14:23.

46. Thus the Whiteheads speak of an "asceticism" of time. See above, pp. 94, 100.

47. For example, Mark 2:17; see Rudolf Bultmann, *The History of the Synoptic Tradition* (Oxford: Basil Blackwell, 1968), pp. 162-168.

48. Matt 10:5-15; Mark 6:7-13; Luke 9:1-6; 10:1-12.

49. See 1 Cor 1:14-17.

50. Cf. Mark 16:14-18.

51. Both in the modern sense of providing "information" (data) and in the scholastic sense of providing form for.

52. See R. F. Collins, *Introduction to the New Testament*, pp. 352-353.

# Chapter Twelve

The Anthropological Model


*Is Christian Ministry Truly Human?*

Reflections on the New Testament Scriptures lead
inevitably to another dimension of theological
reflection, the anthropological correlative.  In the
mission discourse of the Synoptic tradition,[1] it is
clearly stated that the disciples of Jesus have a
function other than that of merely preaching the kingdom
of God.  That function is the function of casting out
demons and healing human ills.  The canonical conclusion
to Mark's Gospel recapitulates the notion that Jesus'
disciples, here typified by the Eleven, are to be
involved in the ministry of exorcism and healing, a
ministry which is interpreted as "a sign which will
accompany those who believe."[2]

That the disciples' ministry of proclamation
should be accompanied by a ministry of exorcism and
healing is merely another way of saying that their
ministry continues the ministry of Jesus of Nazareth
whose life on earth was characterized not only by his
proclamation of the Kingdom but also by his ministry of
healing and casting out demons.  In his description of
the first of the miracles of Jesus, Mark, the author of
the gospel of miracles, described the exorcism worked by
Jesus in the synagogue in Capernaum in such a fashion as
to identify Jesus as one endowed with authority and
hence qualified to teach with authority.[3]

At a deeper level, however, the exorcisms worked
by Jesus are much more than signs of the authority and
authenticity of Jesus' mission.[4]  Rather they are
dramatic proclamations of the kingdom of God.  The Reign
of God, which presently exists in promise, consists in
the effective sovereignty of God over all that is His
creation.  As those who have been possessed are freed
from oppressive demons, the Reign of God is being made
manifest.  Thus the exorcisms of Jesus are the
proclamation, in gesture, of the coming of the Kingdom
of God.

Enlightening, too, is the story of Jesus' healing
of the paralytic.[5]  The rhetorical question points to

the correlation between the "spiritual" and the
"physical" dimensions of Jesus" ministry. "Which is
easier, to say to the paralytic, 'Your sins are
forgiven', or to say, 'Rise, take up your pallet and
walk'?"[6] As proleptically realized in the ministry of
Jesus, the Reign of God is a single complex event.
There is no separation of the transcendent from the
imminent. Jesus is not only interested in the man's
soul; he is also interested in his physical well-being.
The point has been stressed by Schweizer who commented
that: "The real need is exposed by Jesus' answers. It
is not as if this sick man were unusually sinful, but
his case makes the universal separation of man and God
more conspicuous and illustrates the truth which is
proclaimed over and over in the Old Testament, that all
suffering is rooted in man's separation from God. For
this reason, Jesus must call attention here to man's
deepest need; otherwise the testimony of this healing
would remain nothing more than the story of a remarkable
miracle. On the other hand, the second of Jesus'
sayings makes it clear that forgiveness of sins is never
merely a subjective experience, but that it restores the
sovereignty of God even over a man's physical nature."[7]

On the basis of the New Testament evidence,
therefore, the ministry of Jesus as well as the ministry
of his disciples was a ministry in which the religious
and physical components accompany one another as the
total sign of the kingdom of God, proleptically realized
in human history.


*Ministerial Reflection*

When human communication is subject to analysis by
means of the ITT, it is clear that communication is
effective to the extent that a real "impression" is made
on the receiver. The type of impression made on the
receiver derives, at least partially, from the
correlations along the syntactic axis which the receiver
makes with the object of the communication. In the
absence of significant correlations, the intended
communication will be perceived as relatively
unimportant, perhaps even valueless by the receiver.
Accordingly, the communication will make relatively
little, if any, impression upon the receiver.

The phenomenon is well known in the advertising
world. Advertisers appeal to the self-interest of the
prospective customers. They appeal to the customer's

desire for status, economic security, their desire for
the well-being of their children, and so forth. By
appealing in this fashion, advertisers try to present
the product being advertised as something of value to
the receiver of the advertisement (a message). Thus

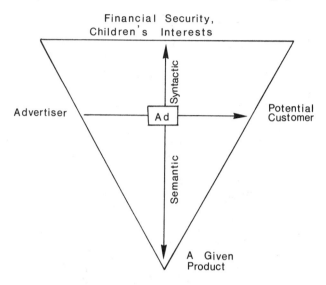

By appealing to the self-interests of their prospective
customers, the advertisers attempt to portray their
product as something of value ( a judgment which
corresponds to the third level of cognition) and induce
the receiver of the advertisement to purchase the
product (move to "responsible" action, on the fourth
level of cognition).

   This example can help to clarify a major pastoral-
ministerial problem for the church in our times. The
church's message is being communicated to its
congregations and the non-church population through the
ministry of its ministers. In order that that ministry
be effective communication, the church's message must be
perceived as something important, as something of value,
by those to whom it is communicated. The receiver must
make a correlation between the sign (a specific
ministerial activity) and the other things of value
which lie along the receiver's syntactic axis.
Effective ministry must appeal to the recipient's value
system; it must correlate with the receiver's world
view.

In times past, the correlation of the church's ministry with the receiver's world view was relatively easy. Commenting upon the success of the church's ministry during the medieval period — despite the sorry state of the church's ministers! — Michael Winter noted that: "basically medieval religion succeeded because it fulfilled a variety of human needs at a time when mankind was fundamentally religious."[8] To a certain extent Christian ministry continued to be successful even after the Enlightenment because the Christian religion was practically perceived as an element of culture and tradition. It was culture and tradition which validated and authenticated the various Christian "signs", including ministerial activity.[9]

With respect to the ITT, it has been noted that the relationship between the sign and its referent along the semantic axis is a matter of the clarity of the sign.[10] The relationship between the sign and the sign system to which it belongs along the syntactic axis is a matter of the consistency and authenticity of the sign. This reflection places the pastoral-ministerial problem of the church in our times in proper focus. "The problem," it has been written, "is how to rethink the Christian faith in a culture each day growing more remote from the circumstances in which the faith originated."[11] If the church's ministry is to be effective, its ministerial activity must cohere and correlate with what its receivers, both the congregation and the non-church world, perceive to be of value. Thus an effective ministry must be one in which the church's ministry "implies" the receiver's value system.[12] In the absence of such correlation, the ministry will not make a (significant) impression. Thus as a paradigm of effective ministry we have:

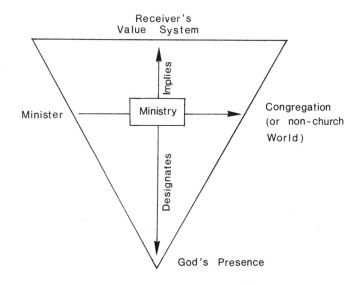

In times past, the popular world view was one which placed the source of value outside the realm of human experience. The real (that is the important or the truly significant) was located in a somewhat Platonic World of Ideas of which present existence was but a faint shadow. The secular was important to the extent that it was touched (blessed) by a supernatural power. This world view provided the context for the popularity of the incarnational model of Christology. Now, however, the world view popular with man come of age locates the important and the truly significant within the realm of human experience. Through science we can understand, and through technology we can control and adapt to our "needs", all that is. Even if we are not able to control all that we see and experience, our optimism is such that we believe we can control all, the only condition being that we make a commitment of our mental and physical resources. We live in an age when the human is king.

This reflection on the context within which the recipient of the church's ministry lives and thinks means that an effective ministry today is one in which the minister will take into account the recipient's existential or lived value system. The minister will attempt to correlate his or her ministry and that value system (an aspect of the receiver's world view), since it is that value system which is the effective interpretive grid for the messages which the receiver receives.

An adequate description of the world view and value system of today's population (the authenticating sign system according to the ITT model) would take us far beyond the possibilities of the present disquisition. As an example of a summary description of the value system of one potential group of receivers of the church's ministry we can once again cite Michael Winter. "The values," he writes, "which young people consider important in life are their personal integrity before loyalty to an institution, justice instead of selfishness, honesty before obedience, security or comfort, the dignity of the person as sacrosanct, and the acceptance of individual's personality as it is."[13] The values esteemed by society as a whole perhaps cannot be identified as readily as the values of the younger generation, but in a general sort of way they are similar to those cited in Winter's "catalogue of values".

Pragmatic reasons, therefore, dictate that the minister of the church appeal to the interests and felt needs of those for whom ministry is intended if the ministry is to be effective.


*A Philosophical and Theological Reflection*

Yet one must ask whether it is *only* because of pragmatic reasons that effective ministry must correlate with the receiver's value, world view, and even self-interest. Might it not even be said that an appeal to these elements of the receiver's signs system is part of the message of the Gospel itself?

As an entry into this type of discussion, we can refer once again to some reflections on the church's mission enunciated by Roger Haight. Haight spoke of the "problem of the Church" as a radical problem insofar as it involves the very basis or reason for being a religious person. Only after that issue has been positively resolved, can one logically raise the question of being a member of the church. He continued:

"Two suppositions underlie this dimension of the problem of the Church. The first is theological and may be expressed baldly in this way: Any Christian doctrine and consequently any understanding of the Church must

enter into and correlate with human experience. ...
theological and doctrinal expressions of faith must
express faith as it is generated in people's lives and
experienced in each age and culture. So central and
fundamental and, in a sense, so obvious is this
principle that it may be stated somewhat categorically
that unless a teaching or doctrine on the Church is
experienced as meaningful and relevant for life in this
world, whether it confirm, confront, or seek to
transform life in this world, it is non-sense.

"The second supposition resides in the cultural
phenomenon that more and more human beings are
experiencing a feeling of being at home in this world
and of responsibility for much of the human condition.
... However distorted by selfish concerns, however
perverted by ignorance, however contradicted in actual
fact by ambiguous decisions, the implicit and constant
desire of men and women today is to build a better world
and a more humane society for all. ...

"If these suppositions be true, then it follows
that any understanding of the Church today must
correlate with the experience that people have of
themselves, of their world, and of the project that they
envisage as possible in and for this world."[14]

Haight's remarks deal with an understanding of the
church, and not with the understanding of the
ministerial activity as such. Ministerial activity is,
however, an expression of the church. It, too, seeks
understanding and that understanding will be had only if
ministry correlates with the experience that people
have of themselves. Indeed, if ministry can be
expressed as a gesticular form of the language of the
Christian faith, then it follows that "the existential
meaningfulness of such language may be described as its
ability to allow for the disclosure of certain modes-of-
being-in-the-world which, *qua*, religious are not trans-
worldly but recognizably and authentically human."[15]

If ministry is the gesticular form of (at least
some aspect of) the Christian message, then one can
speak of a cognitive claim inherent in its message. The
message is a religious one. Its meaningfulness can be
subject to an analysis similar to that which David Tracy
has made with regard to the meaning of metaphysical
statements. In Tracy's judgement, any metaphysical
analysis must meet two general criteria for metaphysical
statements: coherence, and fidelity to experience,
broadly and fairly understood.[16]

If a metaphysical statement, or a religious statement, of which ministry is a gesticular form, is to be understood as meaningful, it must correlate with human experience. In this regard, experience is not only (and not primarily) to be regarded as sense experience or objective experience, but also (and primarily) as the experience of the self-as-self or subjective experience.[17] A religious statement must correlate with one's own experience of the self if it is to be understood as meaningful.[18]

A second criterion to be used in the analysis of a metaphysical or religious statement is its coherence. The cognitive claims of the statement[19] must be able to be expressed logically and coherently. The internal coherence of the cognitive claims allows for the judgement that the statement has meaning.

The application of these two criteria — "meaningfulness as disclosive of our actual experience" and "meaning-as-internal-coherence" as applicable to any cognitive claims — constitute the phenomenological moment in which is disclosed the meaning and meaningfulness of an experience.[20]

But "Even these two criteria combined will not suffice philosophically. In the case of cognitive claims, we want to know not only whether they are meaningful and coherent, but also whether they are 'true'. To respond to that last and most demanding question, one final set of philosophical criteria are demanded. Criteria of 'adequacy to experience'."[21] In other words, to the phenomenological moment of the metaphysical analysis of the religious experience (from the standpoint of the minister, a ministerial experience), there must be added a "trandscendental moment" to disclose the true conditions of the possibility of that experience.[22]

Consequently Tracy speaks of an analysis which demands the application of "three sets of criteria: 'meaningfulness', 'meaning', and 'truth'. A particular experience or language is 'meaningful' when it discloses an authentic dimension of our experience as selves. It has 'meaning' when its cognitive claims can be expressed conceptually with internal coherence. It is 'true' when transcendental or metaphysical analysis shows its 'adequacy to experience' by explicating how a particular concept (e.g., time, space, self, or God) functions as a fundamental 'belief' or 'condition of possibility' of all our experience."[23]

These three criteria are to be applied cumulatively, but it will be readily perceived that a cognitive claim cannot be perceived to be "true", that is, adequate to the totality of experience, if it is not also "meaningful", that is, correlative with and disclosive of experience.[24]

Within this perspective, it is clear that many ministers of the church are involved in ministry that they deem to be "true" in the sense that it discloses something of God's presence in the world. However the ministry in which they are engaged is oftentimes not perceived as true because it is not even "meaningful"; it is not perceived as disclosive of the actual situation of those to whom the ministry is addressed.[25] Accordingly, if ministry is to be effective it must be meaningful. It must correlate with and be disclosive of the actual situation of those to whom it is directed. The practical conclusion which the minister must take from this analysis of "the meaning and meaningfulness of religious language and experience"[26] is that if ministry is to be effectively disclosive of the divine it must correlate with human experience.

## The Biblical Tradition

Were one to turn attention away from the philosophical discussion, from a consideration of the ability of religious language to convey metaphysical truth, to a reflection upon the great symbols of the biblical tradition, one would also arrive at the conclusion that the authentically human, that is, the satisfaction of the needs of human well-being, is not indifferent to the Christian religious tradition.

One could cite, first of all, the theme of God as Creator. The theme is dramatically expressed in the Priestly "myth" of Gen 1-2:4, and the Yahwist "myth" of Gen 2:4b ff. Within the context of the present quest for models of theological reflection, the Genesis creation stories evoke two significant considerations.

On the one hand, they speak of monotheism and a monotheistic world view. By that very fact a dualistic world view is excluded from the Judeo-Christian faith tradition. Within this tradition there can be no spearation of the spirit from matter, no separation of the "religious" from human "well-being". This monotheistic world view has thoroughly formed the

Jewish-Christian perception of reality. By way of example, we can think of the Decalogue. It is a unique reflection of the Jewish world view in that the "first table" of the decalogue speaks of responsibilities to God, while the "second table" speaks of responsibilities to one's neighbors.[27] The divine and human co-ordinates of one's existence cannot be separated from each other. The same perspective is reflected in Jesus' synthesis of the Law in terms of the two great commandments, love of God and love of neighbor.[28] As another example, one could cite the Pauline work ethic. Paul exercised the tentmaker's trade and repeatedly called the attention of his readers to the fact that he earned his own living.[29] Underlying his remarks is not only the fact that he did not want to impair the authenticity of his message by appearing to be a parasite on society, but also the traditional rabbinic understanding that the teacher must also have and be engaged in a trade. This sharply distinguished the Jewish rabbis from contemporary teachers in the Hellenistic world where teachers were to be involved in things of the mind and spirit, the exercise of manual labor being considered as beneath their dignity.[30]

On the other hand, the creation myth identifies the human as the apex of creation.[31] The priestly author of Genesis 1 sees the primal couple as the climax of creation, endowed with vicegerency over all else that has been created. Humans are to express their "likeness" to God by using creation to their own ends. The Yahwist author of Genesis 2 portrays man as he has come from the hand of the Creator in a situation of ease and comfort, as symbolized by the oasis of Eden. Yahweh deems to take away his solitude by creating a companion for the Man in the person of the Woman. That animals are for man's use is symbolized by Adam's naming them. In sum, both of the Genesis creation myths point to human well-being as the fulfillment of the creation story.

Another major symbol taken from the biblical tradition is that of Yahweh as Lord of History. The principal experience of salvation within the history of Israel was the Exodus event. It resulted in the amphictyonic union of the tribes, the independence of Israel, and the possession of the land. It was experienced as an event of redemption and constitution. Associated with the Exodus event was the use of the covenant (*berith*) motif to express the relationship between Yahweh and Israel, his people. The great covenant gift was *shalom*, peace. To *shalom* corresponded neither the philosophical notion of the tranquility of order nor the political notion of the absence of war and violence. Both of these notions were, however, subsumed into the idea of *shalom*, an umbrella term to designate the total well-being of Yahweh's people.[32] *Shalom* even includes the physical and social aspects of well-being: abundant crops, many and healthy children, a beautiful wife, and so forth.

Still another biblical symbol is that of Jesus himself, to which reference has already been made. When the law of the Incarnation is taken in its fullest sense,[33] it will be seen that the Incarnation represents the embrace of the human by God. Jesus is the human face of God, the one in whom the divine disposition is transparent. What one sees in Jesus is not only a divine concern for the "salvation of souls," but also a manifestation of the divine concern for the well-being of men and women. In the compassion which motivated the feeding of the four thousand[34] can be seen the compassion of God. Luke's programmatic statement about the significance of Jesus' ministry is that the prophetic Spirit descended upon Jesus, not only in order that he proclaim the good news, but also in order that he minister to human needs: "'The Spirit of the Lord is upon me, because he has anointed me to preach the good news to the poor. He has sent me to proclaim release to the captives and recovery of sight to the blind, to set at liberty those who are oppressed, to proclaim the acceptable year of the Lord'.... Today this Scripture has been fulfilled in your hearing."[35]

In sum the dominant models of the Christian biblical tradition reflect a God who is concerned with the material and spiritual well-being of men and women. He is not a God who is indifferent to human need. God reigns, that is, the kingdom of God is realized, insofar as the situation of human want and need is satisfied. This aspect of the reign of God must be transparent in the ministry of those who consider the church to be a sign of the kingdom of God.

### The Sacramental System

To speak of signs within the church is to evoke the sacraments, traditionally considered as signs which effect what they signify, as signs which express the very nature of the church.[36] There are various ways of looking at the seven sacraments, traditionally

203

identified as constituting the sacramental system of the church. One of these ways is to look at the sacraments as responding to some of the fundamental needs of the human person.[37]

We can begin with Baptism. It corresponds to the human need for belonging. Every human being needs a community as a significant frame of reference. This need is experienced all the more acutely in our times when so many people are condemned to the isolation of anonymous existence in the apartments of the high-rises of our major cities. Baptism is also a symbol of affirmation. Each human person suffers from an insecurity which comes from an uncertainty as to whether he or she will be accepted as he or she really is, once faults and foibles are known. Baptism is the sacrament of God's unqualified and gratuitous acceptance. It is the sacrament of affirmation, par excellence. Indeed, the affirmation-conferring aspect of baptism is additionally implied by the fact that baptism confers a mission upon the baptized. The baptized person is indeed worthwhile, he or she has something to do, a mission to be accomplished.

Confirmation is the sacrament of Christian maturity, the sacrament of Christian adulthood. It satisfies the human need for "rites of passage".[38] Sophisticated moderns tend to look upon the rites of passage of the various indigenous cultures with a bit of disdain, considering them to be outmoded rituals of a primitive society. A closer look at contemporary western society will allow the perceptive observer to see that we, too, have our "rites of passage". These significant rites in our cultures go by such names as "first date", "high school graduation",[39] "acquisition of driver's license", and so forth. As the completion of baptism, confirmation signifies that the Christian has come of age and is to be involved in the mission of the church.[40]

The Eucharist is the third of the sacraments of initiation, and the culmination of the process. The Eucharist satisfies the human need of celebration. It corresponds to our need for community. In the midst of everyday experience, we often feel the need to celebrate. When a natural occasion is not indicated on the calendar, we will frequently invent a "reason" to celebrate. When we celebrate, and when we express our belonging to a community, we normally do so in the context of shared food and drink. We have our traditional Christmas dinners, the meals of our family

204

get-togethers, and the cocktail parties which grace our calendars.

The sacrament of orders symbolizes service and ministry within the church. As a sign to those towards whom ordained ministerial service is directed, the sacrament of orders speaks of our need to be served, our need of assistance, and our need to know that service is available when we need it. People who are away from home know full well the feelings of alienation, insecurity, and frustration that come when they don't know how and where to obtain service, even in such simple matters as getting one's auto or television repaired. Moreover, the sacrament of orders speaks also to our need for a structured community.

Marriage is a sacrament likewise ordered, indeed explicitly so, to the satisfaction of human needs. It creates a context in which sexual needs are met. It satisfies the human need for intimacy. It takes away loneliness and corresponds to the social aspects of one's personal existence. Marriage satisfies the need of the human race to be continued; it provides young people to ensure the vitality and functions of the race. As a celebration, it corresponds to our need to proclaim that "we are in love." How eager are we to tell the world when we have fallen in love!

Penance satisfies our need to speak about evil, indeed about its mysterious and superhuman power. It corresponds to our need for cleansing, our need for wholeness. It corresponds to our need to come to grips with our guilt, to share it openly with another who will not reject us. Penance satisfies our need for forgiveness, and for the assurance that we are indeed forgiven.

Finally, the sacrament of anointing speaks of our need to be affirmed when we are least able to be a contributing member of the community. When we are seriously ill we often experience a loss of face, and sometimes a loss of value, because we are infirm and are not able to contribute to others. In such circumstances we feel somewhat alienated from our community, because we cannot participate in it. The cards, flowers, and visits that we receive are so many signs that, after all, we are worthwhile despite our inability to contribute; that we belong in spite of the fact that we cannot participate vigorously. The sacrament of anointing is the affirmation by the Christian community of its weakest members. It is the consoling and

205

affirming visit of the community to the sick in the person of its official minister.

It would be a mistake to limit our understanding of the sacraments to so many ecclesial gestures which satisfy human needs. On the other hand, it is equally narrow to consider the sacraments exclusively in their "religious" aspects as if that which they signified did not also embrace the concern of the Church and of Jesus its Lord for human well-being, in the totality of it. Indeed the sacraments, as most characteristic signs of the church's ministry, signify that authentic ministry of the church also embraces a concern for the total well-being of humans.

## A Brief Reflection

When we consider the anthropological model as the fifth of an interlocking series of models of theological reflection, we should bear in mind that theology and anthropology are closely interrelated. The understanding of God implies an understanding of what it means to be human and vice versa. The relationship between theology and anthropology has been given a somewhat extreme expression in the writings of Bultmann[41] and Bonhoeffer[42] who virtually equate theology with anthropology. In a more moderate form, the relationship is expressed in the works of Karl Rahner who considers an understanding of man to be the starting point for true theological reflection. The anthropological concern was also patent in the works of Avery Dulles and John O'Grady whose writings provided the cadre for the ecclesial and christological models presented in these pages. For Dulles, "correspondence with religious experience of men of today"[43] is among the criteria for a meaningful understanding of the church, while O'Grady considers that "the ability to foster a good sense of Christian anthropology"[44] is an important criterion for a meaningful Christology. "The more we can understand ourselves, the more we can understand Jesus."[45]

If anthropology has an important role to play in the development of a contemporary theology, it has an even more important role to play in theological reflection whose material object is a ministerial, but human, experience. If anthropology can function as a criterion for evaluating, that is, judging such major theological disciplines as ecclesiology and Christology, it should also function as a criterion for evaluating a ministerial experience. In the judgment of Harvard's Gordon Kaufman, experience is to be located at the conclusion of reflection, it functions as a final check on the accuracy of the reflection.[46]

In effect, one's experience of what is means to be authentically human is a dominant feature of the syntactic axis along which the receiver perceives the significance of a ministerial sign

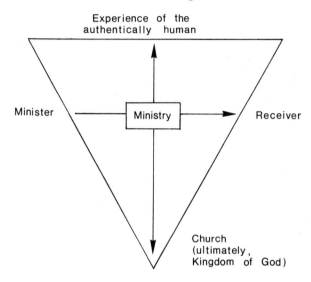

When the ministerial sign is consistent with, and hopefully promotes, the authentically human it is perceived by the one(s) to whom it is directed as being truly of value. In this sense, the experience of what is authentically human[47] serves as a validation of the ministerial experience. When, however, a ministerial sign is perceived by those to whom it is directed (or those who witness it) as inconsistent with the authentically human or detrimental to it, the ministerial sign is perceived as valueless, perhaps even as a major disvalue.[48]

The affirmation of the anthropological correlative as an essential part of theological reflection represents, in fact, a meeting of two different approaches to the task of theological reflection. Earlier it had been noted that one might proceed from *theoria* to *praxis* or from *praxis* to *theoria*.[49] If one proceeds from our theological and biblical tradition, then it is clear that the God of revelation, and his paradigmatic ministers,[50] are concerned with the true welfare of human beings. If one proceeds from communications theory in an attempt to understand   the meaning of the messages that are being sent, one concludes that these messages must correlate with human experience if they are to be perceived as authentic signs, let alone as authentic signs of the transcendent among us.

In a sense we have come full circle. We have started with a reflection on experience and have returned to experience as a criterion for evaluating those particular experiences that we call religious, pastoral, or ministerial. Could it be otherwise when we are dealing with a ministry of human to other humans? Could it be otherwise when His name is Emmanuel?[51]

1.  Matt 10:1-16; Mark 3:13-19; 6:8-11; Luke 9:1-6; 10:1-12.

2.  Mark 16:9-20, esp. v. 17.  Paul also speaks of the "signs of a true apostle" (2 Cor 12:12).  See C. K. Barrett, *The Signs of an Apostle* (London: Epworth, 1970), esp. p. 122, n. 80.

3.  Mark 1:21-28; see Luke 4:33-37.

4.  The notion that the works of Jesus are signs of the authenticity of his mission is one dimension of the Johannine understanding of the *semeia* of Jesus, a dimension to which  Bultmann, in particular, has called attention.

5.  Mark 2:1-12; par. Matt 9:1-8; Luke 5:17-26.

6.  Mark 2:9.

7.  Eduard Schweizer, *The Gospel according to Mark* (Richmond: John Knox, 1970), p. 61.

8.  Michael Winter, *Mission Resumed?* (London: Darton, Longman & Todd, 1979), p. 13.

9.  The American Roman Catholic experience is a good witness to this phenomenon.  The degree of participation in church activity is higher in "ethnic parishes" than in those of modern suburbia.  In the ethnic parishes participation in the rituals of the church is intimately related  to  the preservation of the cultural heritage.

10. See above, p. 80.

11. See *Agenda for Prophets* (London: Bowerdean Press, 1980).

12. In contemporary America, parents place great value on the well-being and success of their children. For this reason commercial advertisements appeal to children and their well-being — with remarkable success.  In parallel fashion, religious educators have been successful in involving adults in religious education programs, when they participate as parents in programs appended to the sacramental initiation of their children.  More basically, pastors have noted that a number of young adults, who have not been formally involved in the life of the church since university days "return to the

church" once they have begun to raise a family.

13. M. Winter, *Mission Resumed?*, p. 33.

14. R. Haight, *art. cit.*, pp. 621-622. Haight cites Rahner's *Shape of the Church to Come* (London: Darton, Longman & Todd, 1974) as a work in which this notion appears as a major theme.

15. D. Tracy, *op. cit.*, p. 146.

16. *Idem.*, p. 172. Cf. Antony Flew, *God and Philosophy* (New York: Harcourt, Brace and World, 1966), pp. 27-29; Schubert M. Ogden, "The Task of Philosophical Theology," in *The Future of Philosophical Theology*, 65-72, pp. 71-72.

17. See D. Tracy, *op. cit.*, p. 69.

18. *Idem.*, p. 172, with reference to the "turn to the subject", made famous by Bernard Lonergan's *The Subject* (Milwaukee: Marquette University Press, 1968). See D. Tracy, *op. cit.*, p. 191, n. 2.

19. In terms of the earlier analyses by means of the ITT, this would at least imply coherence between the ministerial sign and the minister's sign system along the syntactic axis.

20. See D. Tracy, *op. cit.*, p. 69.

21. *Idem.*, pp. 70-71.

22. *Idem.*, p. 69.

23. *Idem.*, p. 71.

24. On the distinction and relationship between experience and verification, see Bernard Lonergan, *Insight*, p. 671. For Lonergan, verification is "a reflective grasp of the unconditioned that grounds every other judgment."

25. On the contrary, the success of Liberation Theology in Latin America is due to the fact that it correlates with the experience of Christians in that area of the world at the present time.

26. D. Tracy, *op. cit.*, p. 146.

27. From an exegetical standpoint, the two tables of

Deut 5:22 most probably indicate two copies of the entire Decalogue. Here, however, we have adopted the language of the catechetical tradition (as old as Augustine) which associates three precepts with the first table of the Law, and the other seven commandments with the second table of the Law.

28. Mark 12:29-33; par. Matt 22:37-39.

29. For example, 1 Thess 2:9.

30. See further Ronald F. Hock, "The Workshop as a Social Setting for Paul's Missionary Preaching," *The Catholic Biblical Quarterly* 41 (1979) 438-450; *The Social Context of Paul's Ministry. Tentmaking and Apostleship* (Philadelphia: Fortress, 1980).

31. At least three different literary motifs point to the climactic function of the creation of humans: (1) the pre-meditation of Gen 1:26; (2) the creation of humans on the final day of the divine "work week"; and, (3) the announcement that it was "very good" (v. 31, in comparison with the simple "good" of vv. 12, 25).

32. Edwin M. Good has described *shalom* as follows: "The state of wholeness possessed by persons or groups which may be health, prosperity, security, or the spiritual completeness of covenant. In the OT no particular distinction is made among these categories; military or economic peace is similar to the bodily and spiritual health of the individual." In a similar vein, Xavier Léon-Dufour has written: "It also indicates the well-being of daily existence, the state of the man who lives in harmony with nature, with himself, with God. Concretely, it is blessing, rest, glory, riches, salvation, life." See E. M. Good, "Peace in the OT," *Interpreter's Dictionary of the Bible*, 3 (Nashville: Abingdon, 1962) 704-706, pp. 704-705; Xavier Léon-Dufour, "Peace," in *Dictionary of Biblical Theology* (London: Geoffrey Chapman, 1969) 364-367, p. 364.

33. That is, not in the limited sense of the Incarnational model of Christology. See above, pp. 151-152.

34. Mark 8:1-10, v. 2; see Matt 15:32.

35. Luke 4:18-19 (Isa 61:1-2), 21. See R. F. Collins,

"Luke 3:21-22, Baptism or Anointing," *The Bible Today* 84 (1976) 821-830.

36. See above, p. 29.

37. This approach has been followed by Frank Sheed (*Theology and Sanity*, London: Sheed and Ward, 1948), George McCauley (*Sacraments for Secular Man*, New York: Herder and Herder, 1969), E. J. Fiedler and R. B. Garrison (Chapter One of *The Sacraments: An Experiment in Ecumenical Honesty*, Nashville: Abingdon, 1969), J. D. Crichton ("The Sacraments and Human Life" in *Christian Celebration: The Sacraments*, London: Geoffrey Chapman, 1974, pp. 31-38), and Bertrand de Margerie (*Sacrements et développement intégral*, Paris: Téqui, 1976).

38. See John Dreher, "Confirmation: Coming of Age," *The Homiletic and Pastoral Review* 70 (1970) 505-512.

39. A report by John Hanlon in the *Providence Journal* in the fall of 1981 told the story of a successful United States magistrate who dropped out of high school during World War II in order to join the army. Even at the conclusion of university studies and after the acquisition of his law degree and the pursual of a successful career he still longed for the missing high school diploma.

40. There is considerable reflection to be brought to bear upon the relationship between the sacrament of Baptism and the sacrament of confirmation. To the extent that the two are separated, one can see in confirmation the specificity of the gift of the Spirit empowering unto mission. See R. F. Collins, "Confirmation: A Theological Overview," *The Homiletic and Pastoral Review* 70 (1970) 603-609.

41. See R. Bultmann, *The Theology of the New Testament*, 2 vols, (London: SCM, 1968-1970).

42. Cf. D. Bonhoeffer, *Christology* (London: Collins, 1971).

43. A. Dulles, *Models of the Church*, p. 181.

44. J. F. O'Grady, *op. cit.*, p. 172.

45. *Ibid.*

46. See G. Kaufman, *An Essay on Theological Method*

(Missoula: Scholars Press, 1975).

47. The notion of "authentically human" implies a
critical anthropology. The limited purpose of the
present work precludes extensive disquisition upon
the idea of the authentically human. Certainly not
every felt need is an authentic need of the human
person, which ought to be satisfied in order that
human well-being be promoted. Moreover it cannot
be presumed that every scientific   and
technological advance necessarily promotes human
progress and well-being.

Elements taken from philosophical ethics and
from Christian moral theology should be introduced
into the discussion of what is authentically human.
From a biblical perspective John O'Grady and Jerome
Murphy-O'Connor have developed notions of Christian
anthropology. See J. F. O'Grady, *Christian
Anthropology* (New York: Paulist, 1976) and
J. Murphy-O'Connor, *Becoming Human Together*
(Wilmington: Michael Glazier, 1977). See further
*Louvain Studies* 5:1 (1974-1975) 1-88.

An adequate notion of the "authentically
human" must certainly include the realization that
the human person exists in time and space. Every
human being has a history and belongs to a society.
These elements must be part and parcel of any
anthropology which is used as an element of
critique in theological reflection. Many well-
intentioned pastoral initiatives have proven to be
failures in the long run because they failed to
provide for the integration of a "Christian
experience" into the future of the participants'
personal stories and their real-life communities.
Often young people who have been involved in a Teen
Encounter with Christ (TEC) or adults who have
participated in a Cursillo weekend have experienced
no small amount of frustration when they have found
no receptive community into which they can bring
their newly released, but previously pent-up,
emotions along with their newly found ministerial
élan. Alas, their last state is often worse than
their former state. See Matt 12:45, Luke 11:26.

48. The dichotomy has allowed Marx and the classic
Marxists to speak of religion as the opium of the
people. Interestingly, liberation theology has
tried to provide a theological paradigm for the
struggle of the oppressed. This has led to a type

of neo-Marxism insofar as Christians and Marxists
are allied in a common struggle or insofar as a new
form of Christian Marxism has been developed.

49. See above, pp. 41-42.

50. In the sense of such "models" of ministry as
    Elijah, Elisha, Jesus, and Paul.

51. Matt 1:23.  See Matt 28:20.

## Epilogue

This book has been called "Models of Theological Reflection." It might have called, just as appropriately, "Making Sense of Ministry" or "Is Ministry Truly Theological?" The reader who has taken the time to peruse these pages will have surely remarked that different models have been passed in review. Just as surely the reader will have noted that these "models" do not all belong to the same level.

In the first part of the book, we dealt with certain notions of epistemology, notions which must be at least implicit in our reflection if we are to understand anything at all, notions, therefore, which must be part of our reflection if we are truly to understand ministry. Ministry does not generally take the form of verbal propositional statements. Ministry belongs rather to the order of the speaking word. Hence we introduced the model of kinesics, in order to reflect on the fact that physical gestures convey a message and that this message is sometimes at odds with the spoken word. This realization led us to further analyze the human process of conveying meaning. The models of semiotics reminded us that the conveying of meaning is one single process, in which all elements must somehow cohere if there is to be a truly human communication. The schema of the Information Theory Triangle allowed us to consider ministry as a sign and raise the question of how this sign conveyed its meaning.

The models of these three types, epistemological, kinesic, and semiotic provided the theoretical basis for our subsequent reflection. Notions drawn from our brief analysis of these three models permeated the exposition of the five models which served as the focus of interest in the second part of this book. These five models do not, however, all belong to the same level. The efficiency model was reviewed because so much so-called theological reflection has been limited to the merely phenomenological. Much was apparently changed in the years after Vatican II, but so little was actually changed. A study of the efficiency model allowed us to conclude that the change was often on the surface, not in the heart, and that such superficial change often conveyed a message quite contrary to that intended by the Fathers of the Council.

This reflection allowed us to get to the heart of

215

the matter and to evaluate ministry in terms of the touchstone of Christian theology, the community's faith in Jesus Christ. Concretely the community of faith is the church, but the church is an equivocal reality — not only because there are large and small faith communities, not only because there are faith communities of different Christian confessions, but also because there are different understandings of what it means to be a faith community. Christian ministry and the meaning of it is correlative to these different models of church. Then, when we move from the experience of faith in community to Jesus Christ, the object of faith, we must acknowledge that there have been different christologies in the church ever since the time of Peter and Paul. Different christologies continue to be part of the ecclesial experience today. These different christologies often cross confessional lines, but they always dictate different forms of ministry. Accordingly it is good for the church and its ministers to reflect on the Christology which really undergirds its ministry. Frequently the operative Christology may be at odds with the Christology which is verbally professed by the church.

The last models which we examined arose from the critical function of theology. Are the models of church and the understanding of Jesus Christ which dictate the forms of ministry which we embrace the most authentic forms of ecclesiology and Christology? We thought it wise to introduce the Scriptures and human experience as models to criticize not only ecclesiology and Christology but also the forms of ministry which have been developed in function of specific ecclesiologies and specific Christologies. By using the Scriptures and ordinary human experience in this way we brought ourselves back to some of the theoretical notions which had been introduced into the theoretical part of this book. For centuries theology has looked to the Scriptures and the experience of the church (and others as well) as sources for its theologizing efforts. More recently a theologian such as David Tracy has suggested that correlation with the documents of tradition and correlation with common human experience are essential to the (Christian) theological effort.

It is in the belief that ministry must be a word which expresses the Christian faith if it is to be Christian ministry at all that these pages have been written. It is hoped that they have been read in the same spirit, for ministry belongs not only to the category of *praxis*, it must also belong to the category of *theologia*.

"He is in bondage to a sign who uses,
or pays homage to, any significant
object without knowing what is
signifies.  He, on the other hand,
who either uses or honors a useful
sign divinely appointed, whose force
and significance he understands, does
not honor the sign which is seen and
temporal, but that to which all such
signs refer."

Augustine of Hippo
(On Christian Doctrine III, 9, 13)

# Index

221